Mudroor ~~Narogin,~~ Mudrooroo, 1938- ~~a~~nd
has since The kwinkan ·ld.
Mudroor ber
of the Aboriginal Arts Unit committee of the Australia Council, and
was a co-founder with Jack Davis of the Aboriginal Writers, Oral
Literature and Dramatists' Association. He has also piloted Aboriginal literature courses at Murdoch University, the University of
Queensland, the University of the Northern Territory and Bond
University. Mudrooroo is a prolific writer of poetry, prose and
criticism. His first novel, *Wild Cat Falling*, was published in 1965.
Doin' Wild Cat was first published in 1988, and *Wildcat Screaming*
in 1992.

IMPRINT

the K Winkan

by

MUDROOROO

Angus&Robertson
An imprint of HarperCollins*Publishers*

AN ANGUS & ROBERTSON BOOK
An imprint of HarperCollinsPublishers

First published in Australia in 1993 by
CollinsAngus&Robertson Publishers Pty Limited (ACN 009 913 517)
A division of HarperCollinsPublishers (Australia) Pty Limited
25-51 Ryde Road, Pymble NSW 2073, Australia

HarperCollinsPublishers (New Zealand) Limited
31 View Road, Glenfield, Auckland 10, New Zealand

HarperCollinsPublishers Limited
77-85 Fulham Palace Road, London W6 8JB, United Kingdom

National Library of Australia
Cataloguing-in-Publication data:

Mudrooroo, 1938
  The Kwinkan.

  ISBN 0 207 17944 1.

  I. Title.

A823.3

Cover illustration by Greta Kool
Typeset by Midland Typesetters, Maryborough, Victoria.
Printed in Australia by Griffin Paperbacks

5 4 3 2 1
97 96 95 94 93

I respectfully dedicate this book to the linguist, Mari Rhydwen, who helped me with obscure points of Australian/ English usage. Any mistakes are mine. Thanks Mari for your kind and considerate help.

Transcriber's Note

This volume contains the transcripts of thirteen curious recording sessions conducted over the month of July 1992 in the old federal capital of Canberra. They have been edited to delete many hesitations, as well as extraneous and libellous matter, though in the interests of veracity, the oral style of the material has been retained as much as possible. The object of the editing process was to put together a clear, readable manuscript which might go towards elucidating the life and career of the famous Dr Watson Holmes Jackamara. I stress here, as I must, that the name of the subject who subsequently suffered a nervous breakdown and disappeared shortly after the conclusion of the recording sessions, is not to be found in my text. This was at his own request and to preserve his privacy. The manuscript was vetted by both the governments of Australia and of the island nation. Any matters which might directly or indirectly contravene the respective secrecy Acts of both countries have been removed. The unedited tapes are to become part of the Jackamara papers which when collated will be deposited in the Petersen Library of Caine University, Brisbane. There they shall be available for limited perusal by scholars after a period of total restriction as yet to be determined.

SESSION ONE

'Yes, well I did know, or should that be, I do know Detective
Inspector Watson Holmes Jackamara, and I have read, or let
us say glanced through the volume of his exploits, or perhaps
I should say cases. And you are the, the chronicler of his life?
I find it very interesting, most interesting; but what has it got
to do with me? You see, as I did know the Inspector I was
ready to peruse the book and did, but, to be precise, I thought
that you fictionalised the cases too much, not as to the
sensational aspects, but as to appearing to get into the minds
of the participants in the tragedies. I see by your raised eyebrows
that you are querying my use of the word "tragedy"? Well,
sir, I do prefer the formality, I have no wish to extend this
brief meeting into friendship, I regard all police cases as
tragedies, the result of individual strivings and aspirations
colliding with the social mores which may be seen as fate.
Social collapse averted by individual collapse and so it goes
on. I find little of this in your fictionalised working over of
the participants. Well, it is only what must be expected, for
after all, and for that matter how could you really begin to
delve into and understand the inner workings of not fictional
characters, but real people engaged in the tragedy of life often
to such a degree that they put their all on the line. Perhaps
only the policeman, the avenging fury, might begin to
understand and love aspects of the criminal; but not all, sir,
no, not all for after all he is no psychoanalyst; but then what
has psychology got to do with the understanding of a human
nature enmeshed in tragedy? Ah, so you interview people?
Interesting, and the details of the cases? . . . from the Inspector
himself. I remember, even now, that he was an excellent
raconteur. In fact, I feel that I am ready to cooperate in your,
well, in your project of literary realisation.

'I remember Jackamara, I'm sorry, Detective Inspector Watson Holmes Jackamara. It was like this. At that time, I was standing for election to the federal Parliament and he was detailed not only to be my minder, but to pull the black vote onto my side. You see, well, I can admit it now, I was very much the city slicker. Still am for that matter, but, well, you may ask, what has this got to do with my connection with the Detective Inspector? What, you say that he is now a Doctor of Criminology! Well, well! It appears in this world only I remain constant and on the down turn . . . Well, when I met the good Doctor, the black vote was substantial, very substantial in that electorate. It was decided by those in power that I go around to the various settlements and missions to present a sympathetic ear to their grievances. Naturally, I was to promise nothing; but in those days in Queensland the mere presence of a parliamentary candidate amongst the blacks was like the visit of royalty. Still, I needed an "in" and so the Inspector was provided for that "in". We got on splendidly, well, we did to a certain extent, as much as it was possible for a white and black man to get on. He was a great one for the stories, and as our enforced companionship wore away his reserve, he gave me much enjoyment on the road to some of those missions which are so remote that to say out of sight is out of mind is quite correct. Why, he even took me to his old mission home.

'By that time, I was used to these clusters of abandoned humanity lurking on the very brink of my vision. To enter into one of these clusters was a trial. The blacks were stand-offish, preferring to gaze away rather than towards, and the white persons in charge were little better. They on the whole were suspicious of politicians. Some, I saw, had identified almost wholly with their charges; others lorded it over them, and the rest, the majority, suffered their isolation and were ready to fling their petty grievances towards me. Naturally, I ducked them.

'Jackamara's home was typical of these abandoned missions. The better ones had been ordered by the State Government to become municipalities; others like his, a few dilapidated houses squared about a church and a rambling bungalow, the once home of the missionary, were placed under the control of a government agent and forgotten. When I arrived, I found that the agent had taken leave of absence. His headquarters, the bungalow, lay silent behind a mesh fence topped by barbed wire. A light-skinned lad pulled forlornly at the hasp of a heavy padlock securing the gate.

'We alighted from our vehicle in the dusty square. Not a soul in sight except that kid pulling on the lock. Then, then there erupted from between two houses a group of men beating the ground with sticks and yelling, "Snake, snake!" I stared at them nervously, then with a slight grin of derision as I saw the serpent they were after slithering towards us. I could recognise a harmless grass snake when I saw one. I stood there as they approached. Then one of them quickly stooped, grabbed the snake by its tail and flung it at me. I caught what I considered a harmless serpent and held it up. They came forward warily. I looked down at my catch, then gave a start. My God, it was a deadly brown snake. I flung it from me with a gasp of horror. The men watched it disappear under a house— then turned to us.

'Jackamara was amongst his mob and went from man to man explaining my mission. It seemed that handling the snake had been a test of some sort and one which I had passed. We, or rather I, was allowed to camp on the porch of the deserted church for the night. Jackamara got the camp set up while I sat on the camp chair. Individual men approached to sound me out. I hummed and hawed in my usual fashion as I blathered my way through the usual requests; I stated strongly that I was in the running for Minister of Aboriginal Affairs, and agreed to carefully consider each and every problem when I was elected and entered the Ministry. I even made a show of taking notes.

'Finally, and as the sun disappeared beneath the dust and the darkness flickered with the flames of our fire, I left my chair and sat on the porch steps to watch Jackamara preparing supper. A huge billy of tea hung above the flames. By the time it was bubbling, men had appeared from the darkness and settled about the fire. Soft voices murmured and tired with, with keeping up the pretence of wishing to help these people who were as alien to me as I was, I am sure, to them, I fell into a doze . . . I came out of it and into a story being narrated by Jackamara.

'A remarkable story, quite remarkable. It stays in my mind, stays in my mind as much as she stays there. No, she has little to do with this, has little bearing . . . Is that tape-recorder running? Remarkable things, tape-recorders. You could say that they tap the stream of consciousness; but, sir, remember, keep it clearly in mind that I retain the right to vet all material and, and nothing must allude to my identity. Remember the laws of libel. You see I still have enemies. Yes, even now when I am at a low level in my, in my career, and that is why I . . . Well, why should I record my, my downfall, when you are only interested in that black policeman? . . . But, remember, once, then, I could have become the Minister of Aboriginal Affairs and have had him at my beck and call. Alas, it was never to be.

'Jacky, as I called him, was still a simple detective then. Perhaps not so simple as you depict in your case histories; but in those days few appeared ready to acknowledge his uniqueness. It is still hard for me to believe that you have not made up most of those so-called cases, though, no, in hindsight . . . Well, now he has a reputation second to none in the history of the Queensland Police Force. He well deserves that honorary doctorate, and perhaps in one of your future volumes you will detail what must have been a very impressive ceremony . . . Sorry, sorry, I know that I digress. I am forever digressing. My life is one long digression; but, sir, over the years things have not gone right with me. The story? Yes, the story. It seems but last night. There sits Jacky at the fireside. How mysteriously his dark face and the dark faces of his mob glow in the flickering flames as he begins to relate an anecdote which I then took as rank superstition.

'He declared that it had happened when he was a young kid

4

and that his Uncle Willy could vouch for every word. He looked across the fire at a stolid bloke whose eyes reflected red and mysterious from the flames. This man, I knew must be Uncle Willy, and he nodded his shaggy head in verification. As Jackamara flicked his glance towards me, I too found myself nodding, then he went on addressing his words to me, his gaze flickering at times to Uncle Willy at salient points . . . And the story? Well, it is as good a beginning as any for this tape. It seems that once as Uncle Willy and his maternal grandfather, I forget his name if I ever knew it, were walking through the bush in the early evening, a *min min* light came floating towards them. The old man ignored it and kept on walking, but the uncle, he slowed down a bit. He hung back as the old man strode on. In fact, Uncle Willy, it seems, was not one to put his best foot forward and hung back so far that he was at a safe distance when the light flared into a beautiful woman with long flowing hair. He watched from a distance as she spoke to the old man. He saw him go off with her towards a low hill which was a pile of boulders and rock slabs. "It's what you fellows call The Devil's Marbles," Jackamara informed me, and I recalled that he had pointed the hill out to me when we passed it on the way in.

'Uncle Willy didn't have to be told that it was what the local Aborigines call a *Gyinggi* woman, I see you nod at this, and that she had sung, you know what that is, the old man and forced him to follow her to her home in the rocks. In fact, the hill, which the Inspector offered to stop at on the morrow, had a bad reputation and was taboo to the local blacks. They said it was the haunt of spirits, of spirits called *Kwinkan*. Except they are not spirits, for that *Gyinggi* woman when she enchanted men drained the very flesh from their bones until they became stick-like beings. Uncle Willy didn't want this to happen to the old man, so he rushed off back to the mission for help. Half-a-dozen men reluctantly came back with him, urged on by an old bloke who believed that he had the necessary, I suppose you might call it, medicine to force a passage through to the *Gyinggi* woman and her prey. By the time they reached the foot of the hill, it was almost pitch black. They saw a light glowing halfway up the slope and carefully they climbed to it. Hard work it was, for it was no joke making your way across those piled-up rocks in the dark. Finally, they reached a huge tree emerging from the slabs of rock. It had pushed aside the slabs and the light came from underneath one of the tilted slabs. The old fellow mumbled a chant of some sort and came creeping towards the light waving a bunch of feathers, which, it seemed, dislodged any spirit which might be lurking in the branches of the tree ready to spring down on them. They reached that slab and peered beneath. The old man lay there stretched out seemingly asleep. No one else was in the place, then the strange glow began fading. They dragged the old man out. They shook him to bring him to his senses. He came to snarling and snapping like some wild animal. They had to hold him down. One of them who worked for the medical clinic at the mission, thrust a stick between his teeth and then tied his hands and feet. Well, they carried him back to the mission and kept him locked up in a room. Then one time they go to that room, and you know what? Well, that old grandfather had dug his way out through the floor. A concrete floor mind you. It was the last they saw of him. He had returned to that *Gyinggi* woman and was lost to the men. That was the end of him as a man. Well, at least this is what Jacky told me that night. He went on further and said that such a man taken or lured by those women is sucked dry. He becomes a *Kwinkan*, thin and elongated, living in the rocks and crevasses, afraid to face the light of day and other men. He loses his nerve, just as I've lost my nerve. It can happen to the best and worst of us, mate, the best and worst of us. You better believe it!

'Well, stories are stories and Jacky had a fund of them, and most of them just as meaningless, that's what I thought then, smiling before wondering why he had directed that particular story at me, a soon-to-be-elected member of Parliament, a minister too, and thus on his last visit to this godforsaken mission, for let me assure you that it was that. It was a place made for superstition and I remember clearly that I darted a glance at the stern face of the detective while I asked within: "How come an officer of the Queensland Police Force could believe such rubbish?" . . . but then the answer was real easy, he was an Abo, no offence meant, and that settled the matter for me.

'Well, the tape-recorder is still running and, I've made a start. Why there? No matter, I'll just keep on. You'll have to listen if you want to hear about the time, or the times that Jacky, well to give him his due, Detective Inspector Dr Watson Holmes Jackamara figured in my life. You're the one who gets inside the minds of real people, so you have to listen and get inside mine. Now, don't worry, don't worry, Jackamara is the hero of this tape, and I'll get to him, but well, well, what about my life? You have to pass through some of it to get to him, so you better, better listen, take me along with the good Doctor and then cut and shape it; but, but, I have a veto on the material, on my life as it were. It is my life, I want to keep it mine . . .

'Life, you seem to question. Well, we all develop some sort of philosophy of life. That is if we live long enough. Life, I thought once it was what might be called, other-directed, a force rushing into the future loaded with all things nice for me and you, but especially for me. Well, that was then. The old experience eventually gangs up on you and you get some degree of reality, the reality factor going for you. Well, first of all, if you ask me what is life, I must answer, but from what position do you expect me to answer? As the head of a computer section, a minor bureaucrat to be precise, I might answer that it does not compute; or if you wish I shall refer the matter to my division head. So you see I cannot answer it from my official position; but as a man, a human being talking from experience I may. Oh fuck it, what was the question? What is Life? What is it after all but just bits and pieces of memory caked with some sort of emotional slime? Some are tedious, some exciting, and some, I must admit are even terrifying. Well your friend, Jackamara, played a part in my life and thus created some pieces of my memory. It is these which you expect me to open like a computer file and reveal to you the contents in all their pristine accuracy. Well, mate, it doesn't work like that. I'm not a computer and I expect some, well, let me call it remunerative cash—no cheques please—for my ability to open these files to you.

'What, you say that they have an importance only to you? Well, they are mine by the law of privacy. Intellectual property! I own them, mate. Admit that they are important to me through right of ownership . . . but what about others? The laws of libel protect them. I am not a monad existing only in and for and by myself. So my memories are important not only to you in your function as an eventual narrator, but to me and others as well. I am the archive of such memories; and because they are an archive they have an importance towards forming the public view of contemporary history. You see, mate, then I was standing for a seat in Parliament and on the verge of becoming a minister and more important than that friend of yours. Yes, more important, and so if you want to learn about him, you'll have to pay as you go and learn about me as well . . . And don't smirk, don't even wonder why I am so thin now. So much, so much a *Kwinkan*, a thin stick of a body attached to a thick, misshapen penis. Well, she did for me, mate. It happens to the best and the worst of us, and so it happened to me and it all started from that story of Jacky's. I don't know about you people, you Abos, there's something not quite right about you mob, something different. Underneath the old suit and tie of assimilation there beats the heart of an Abo, but no offence, mate, no offence. Just one of those things which are part of the reality factor, then I am pissed off about everything. There's been little contentment in my life over the last years. But, no worries, eh? Or as my esteemed leader used to say, "Don't you worry about that"; but I do, I do. Might have some kind of health and some kind of job, but everything's not apples, mate. Still, it wasn't always like that, like this. No, it wasn't. No, not at all, and one of these days, when I get myself together, things'll change, will change, you'll see; you'll all see. I'll be on top again!

'Well, the tape's running and I have to start somewhere. No, I have started, got to continue. Well, it was over a decade ago, at the end of one of those boom periods for which the economy of Australia is noted, I found myself at the end of my tether, or almost, for the recession had condemned me to seek out some quick, profitable venture to stave off not bankruptcy, this is in the strictest confidence—I really will have to vet this tape—but imprisonment. It was then after a too hasty deliberation that I decided to cash in my last favour with the heir to the then Premier of Queensland, a man who did not like being reminded of old obligations. He made a quick phone call and shifted me as problem over to the head of his party. He greeted me with a cold smile which in rosier times might have warned me to keep on guard; but times were tough and so I listened to his plan to present me as a candidate in the forthcoming federal elections in an electorate in which I knew no one and no one knew me.

'He assured me that the seat was as safe as houses and that my election was in the bag. Some of the old guard had been caught with their hands in the till and thus new blood was needed. I was supposed to be a pint of that new blood; but, from the very beginnings, ugly rumours hissed through the corridors of power that I was an upstart who, apart from party donations, had little political clout and no savvy. These rumours came to my ears, but the political bosses laughed them away. It happened to all new chums, they declared, and added it was a way the wheat was sifted from the chaff. I accepted their reassurances, as I was certain that I did know politicians and how they conducted themselves in government and towards industry. In fact, I felt that I was just as good or as bad as the best or worst of them and could further my interests with much more discretion. So much for my naivety.

'Next came a solemn interview I had with the horrible Prime Minister of our country who had seized power by ruthlessly splitting a coalition of the conservative forces and by establishing an alliance of convenience with a party masquerading as the friends of the poor and the afflicted. There were no problems here for me. The PM was an old school chum who believed that the public school tie knotted around his withered neck gave him the right to plunder at will. I hoped that he did not remember that, well, I was one of an unselect group who had gained entry into the school through scholarship. He didn't let on. My powerful, rich, old school chum greeted me with an outstretched hand and a warm smile to balance out the ice in his wary eyes. "You see," he exclaimed, "we never forget our friends." He let my hand drop. "You shall be an asset to the party, ministerial material. New blood is needed, new blood," he exclaimed . . .

' "I still have to get myself elected," I replied peevishly, thinking that my business mates were paragons of honesty compared to this lot. Still, this old school chum owed me a favour. On many occasions I had helped him with assignments, though I doubted that this was something he might wish to remember.

' "Never you mind; never you mind," he babbled in the nebulous fashion which was the political gift of Queensland to the rest of Australia. "A formality, a formality," he burbled, flashing me his false teeth and even rubbing his hands together. I stared at him as he chattered on. "No worries, no worries, a safe seat and you'll have every chance of taking it with an increased majority. You are what we have been looking for. Intelligent, charming and, and pleasant. Why, with your rugged looks, you'll capture the ladies. You're lean and hard and these'll add to your appeal in the bush. You'll see . . . You're in already . . . but you must understand the situation, understand what you may and must not say. Simple, I assure you. First past the post too."

'His assurances and the classic buttering-up job failed to ease my doubts. I thought my leanness perhaps bulged with malnutrition. I attempted a warm smile of complicity which fell away as I recalled that a cartoonist on the *Courier* had already caricatured me as one of the five horsemen of the apocalypse of recession. It did not help matters when I recalled that our beloved Prime Minister had been placed in the lead. Grimly, I listened to his advice . . .

' "And above all, no politics! No politics! Leave 'em to the Opposition. They always try to drag in politics and come a cropper. And above all don't get involved; don't get carried away by the side issues. Remember, it is a rural electorate, and the voters are only interested in one issue, and one only: the farm subsidy! Wool prices, wheat sales, land rights, the kangaroo menace—ignore them. The farm subsidy is not only to be continued, but increased—adjusted against the rate of inflation. That's all you need to know. Let your opponents wallow in the swamps of generality, stick to the farm subsidy. Do you know anything about the farm subsidy?"

' "My God," I exclaimed, "I've always been involved in urban property. Why, I've never heard of it before. Should I bone up on it?" I queried.

' "No, no," the PM said hastily. "That won't be necessary. We'll get a few set speeches for you and some questions and answers to read through. These'll be enough. Just stick to 'em and you can't go wrong. And above all—don't improvise! Don't get carried away with personalities or general views. Remember commit yourself to nothing, except of course, the farm subsidy. Commitment is dangerous and a threat to the integrity of the party. You know, between ourselves, don't take it personally, old chap, I'm not reproaching you, but there have been rumours, but . . . " and he smiled knowingly.

'My face had long gone numb in the mist of his waffling. The PM was renowned for concealing his ineptitude behind a fog of generalities, a trait he had inherited from his predecessor; and he had successfully done it again. Now I eased my facial muscles into what I hoped was a smile of, of, well, of complicity. After all we were in the same boat and had to pull in the same direction. This I thought was certain, though as I stared into the face of my old school chum, I had to keep a snarl from my voice. I met innuendo with innuendo.

' "Perhaps, there are other and more pertinent rumours circulating," I stated, as if I was privy to such rumours, though as a new chum, I was denied the corridors of power; but then I had other contacts. "It seems," I stated, "there is the matter of a lack of timing. If the Government hadn't acquiesced in that steep rise in interest . . . "

'He interrupted me with a dry laugh, almost a cough, and said with an air of superior detachment: "We are talking about different things, old chap. You see, I'm covered by my position. Any accusation is a political attack, and as for the interest hike, that is not your concern." Thus, having put me in my place, he swung back to the forthcoming campaign. "You only have to remember the farm subsidy and the adjustment against the rate of inflation which naturally has calculated in it any interest rises. Push that down their ear holes. Don't deviate one iota from it and you'll get the white vote, and as for the black vote . . . "

'That was where your detective came in, of course. Then, after arranging for funds to be forwarded to me, he pressed my hand, offered me the certain luck of the draw, then showed me the door.

'I faithfully followed his advice before I discovered that it was completely worthless. My opponent not only crushed me with a huge majority, but at one time I was in danger of losing my deposit. I attributed this defeat not only to the disastrous economic climate and the saddling of me with an Aboriginal bodyguard which drew prejudice towards me (I was seen as soft on the Abos and therefore against the rural interests), but also to the abysmal scheming of the PM and his failure to come to my rescue when the campaign took on a personal tone and I was reeling under attack from all sides.

'I became a witness to how a victim is set up in this great country of ours. Only Jackamara stood by me. He said that the local blacks were 100 per cent behind me, but demanded a statement on land rights. Not bloody likely! I hummed and hawed and lost even that base. My opponent, a wealthy landowner who had dismissed his black employees when he had to pay them a decent wage, pointed the finger of scorn at me. He became the hero of the piece as he laughingly contrasted conditions on a clapped-out station which had been passed over to the blacks with the thriving nature of his own properties.

' "Yes," he declared, "I admit I have made a somewhat comfortable living from my land . . . but this has come through hard work," he shouted out at the church fetes and sheep sales. "And what I have done, they could do," he yelled in a great shout which echoed in the greedy hearts of all those farmers struggling as much as the blacks were struggling to make a success of their farms.

'Evading the issue, I flung what I considered the reality of the farm subsidy, cents against dollars, which he adroitly turned against me as a hidden means of keeping off the market the property on which the blacks were trying to scrape out a living. He ignored the farm subsidy and concentrated on the sudden rise in beef prices. His posters fashioned like hundred-dollar notes flashed his complaisant face as they screamed: "MONEY COMES FROM LAND WELL WORKED AND MANAGED."

'If only they had stopped and thought, but in the town pubs, his agents shouted drinks all round while they trumpeted: "Well, he knows what he's talking about." Drunken heads would nod into their drinks and soon this man, seen as one of them, was acclaimed with a frenzy which increased by the hour. Who needed a subsidy when beef prices remained steady at the new high? Market forces were triumphant!

'My opponent achieved wellnigh divine status when the Brisbane newspapers exposed certain dealings. Now it was country against city, and his victory was assured. My own past, though not my identification with the city, remained all but buried. I found myself at the head of a small minority on the side of accountability in politics. One evening, towards the end of the campaign, I went into the pub in a small town with Jackamara by my side. It was the usual crowd, good-natured in grog, and they even allowed me time to say a few words from the band platform. As I knew the town was dirt poor, I began speaking on the farm subsidy and how it rose in relation to the official inflation figures. This, I declared, would help the weaker rural sectors in which I unfortunately included the Aborigines.

' "Fuck 'em, they get too much already," someone shouted.

' "This is untrue," I unwisely shouted back. "I have seen how these people live, and by my side is one who can tell you about the third-world conditions."

'This was too much for the men to take. I had unwisely settled on a taboo topic. A glass whizzed by my ear and splattered on the wall behind me. Others followed and I hit the deck. I huddled there fearful as a hail of missiles flashed over me and beer splashed down. Desperately I called for Jackamara, and then other missiles came from the reverse direction. There was a shout of "Get the buggers" and the bar became filled with large black bodies and fists. Jackamara had enlisted the blacks from the segregated black bar to come to my rescue. A running battle ensured huge headlines detailing a "Race Riot". With a bruised face as dark as those of my allies, I saw myself going down to defeat. It was then that I knew that I had been set up: I would never become the Minister of Aboriginal Affairs!

'This became clearer in the final hours of the campaign. My election committee, which at the beginning had been very accommodating, now refused to meet and consider my complaints, or even to plan an alternative strategy. I pressed them to honour their pledges, only to find that there was a serious shortage of funds and rumours that certain moneys had been diverted to buy the black vote. It was then I tried to get in touch with the PM. He was unavailable. At the beginning of my campaign, he had promised to make a whirlwind tour of my electorate, but since then not a single word from him. In desperation, I threatened to go to the media and even tried to plant a few stories which might embarrass, but not harm the election prospects of the party. In return certain newspapers attacked me. It was said that I had sent a truckload of grog to an Aboriginal settlement. Under cover of glib journalese, daggers of wounding allusion slashed out. To the party, I was a lame duck. Real or imaginary polls now revealed that my party would be returned to power; but each and every poll showed that my seemingly safe seat was not only in doubt, but lost owing to my ineptitude. I sat fuming as I crashed to defeat. My only apparent friend at the time was my minder, Detective Inspector Watson Holmes Jackamara, but even he had proved a liability. He, after all, was a blackfellow.

'Well, now I have detailed the first period of acquaintance with that policeman. I doubt that he was privy to the plot; but the sight of him beside me on each and every occasion was an element in my downfall. I must admit I breathed a sigh of relief when his job was over and he returned to Brisbane. It was then, that determined to bare all, I rushed to Brisbane where the PM was holding a victory rally. To my consternation, I received an appointment without delay.

' "My dear, dear chap," he exclaimed, coming to me with his hand outstretched. I should have ignored the touch of that Judas, but beggars can't be choosers, and after all he was the PM. "My dear, dear chap," he repeated, pumping my hand once, then letting it fall like one of my how-to-vote cards. "I'm so sorry, so very sorry, but you would drag in extraneous issues, such as land rights. What on earth made you come down so heavily on the side of the Aborigines! Why, it threatens our whole policy on that question. Upon my word, I thought that you had more sense. Still, I never would have believed it. There was a swing against us all over the country and but for another reversal of coalitions we would be sitting on the Opposition benches. Well, well, I never would have believed it," he said shaking his head. It rankled that my opponent was now a member of his cabinet.

' "Don't give me any of that bullshit," I interrupted him coarsely. "And whose bright idea was that to give me the only Aboriginal detective as a bodyguard?" I shouted, banging my fist down on his ornate desk and making the papers jump. "I was set up like a dummy, don't deny it!"

' "Policy, policy," he murmured. "After all, you had to have credibility with the substantial black vote."

'I shook in fury, clenching and unclenching my fists. In an attempt to pacify me, he offered me a chair, thank God, not a seat, then poured me a drink. I downed the glass in a single gulp before grinding out: "All you bastards are laughing at my expense. Well, we'll see who has the last laugh. I'll expose you for what you are. The whole country'll know of it. We'll see; we'll see. In fact with this reversal of coalition tactic, there might be a case to be brought before the Electoral Commission. Once, yes; but twice?"

'I broke off choking with rage and humiliation. The PM waited a moment, then said: "Please be quiet and listen to me. Please, please. I'll let you in on what happened. We had no way of knowing, or of getting word to you. Strategy was planned and put into operation on a day-to-day basis. You're new to the game and don't know how these things are settled . . . "

'My rage had fallen away and I let him continue. Quietly, he explained: "Your rival, he was proving too strong for us to contain. What could we do? It was by sheer chance that he went against you in the first place. All preliminary polls showed that the result would be close and that the deciding factor would be the black vote. So we used what we considered our trump card and brought in Detective Inspector Watson Holmes Jackamara. Well, we had never considered the amount of prejudice against Aborigines in the district. The farmers are frightened that their land may be alienated from them. So what could we do? Party comes first and your opponent was strong material, cabinet material, just what we needed. Everyone knows him. Very popular, indeed. Just a miscalculation. Sorry about that; but our country needs the strongest government in these somewhat difficult times. I am sure that you would have made a fine Minister of Aboriginal Affairs . . . "

' "Christ," I burst out. "Cut the twaddle, you aren't in the house now. I don't care what the country needs; I know what I need. I relied on you, and now thanks to you I'm finished. I'm overdrawn at the bank not by hundreds but by thousands, and at this very moment my creditors are about to pounce.

They'll skin me alive. I've barely got the price of a decent meal in my pocket and when my credit card is dishonoured, I'll be dishonoured. Christ, can't you see the fix I'm in?"

'The PM was a good sort, perhaps. He draped an arm about my shoulders and said: "You had to get it off your chest and now let me say . . . I'm prepared to offer compensation . . . "

' "Reparation is more like it," I ground out.

' "If you wish it to be so . . . "

' "In full."

' "Completely and utterly."

'He smiled and I scowled back in disbelief. "Government needs good men such as yourself," he stated, as he escorted me to the door. There we shook hands to seal the bargain, whatever it was. I was to go to Canberra where many government departments still remained in those days . . .

'Well, that is that. Quite a bit about Jackamara too. A visit to, to his run-down mission home; an account of an Aboriginal story as from his own lips, and his extricating me from what might have been a nasty situation. You can see from this that my account is valuable and we must settle the worth of its value. There is more to come, and I feel that certain, certain facets of the man should be brought out. I did establish a relationship with your Detective Inspector Dr Watson Holmes Jackamara and this must be of worth to you.

'Why, you ask? Cause, well, you know, then, it was, was, I had been set up and with him keeping tabs on me. And, and this set-up continued and your Detective Inspector Jackamara was there to witness my further humiliation. True indeed. And now he is a doctor and what am I but a lowly clerk. Where is the justice in that, I ask you, where? Now, switch off the tape-recorder. I insist. We must discuss the terms and conditions as well as the payment for further sessions. I refuse to continue, sir, without such sureties . . . '

SESSION TWO

'Did I hear you say something about six of one and half-a-dozen of the other? Well, did you, and what are you inferring, sir? Have you been in touch with Jackamara and is this his, his opinion about me? Look, I have found these old photographs taken during my election campaign. Examine them. See, here I am among your people. I, I support you. I was stouter then, wasn't I? Much stronger. Now too thin, too thin. You know power inflates, loss of power deflates. It's a poison draining the flesh from the bones, just like that *Gyinggi* woman Jackamara went on about. I needed, needed support. I was the only candidate who went to your people and listened to their grievances. I went and sat with him and his people and listened to their troubles. Did my opponent ever mention land rights once during his campaign? No, a resounding, no! And then, there is another thing which must be considered—his part in my downfall! If I were an Aborigine, I would never consider joining the police force. I feel that to be an Aborigine is to be without the system, to be, sir, an outlaw. How could a member of your race become not only a policeman, but a respected member of the Queensland Police and thus a part of the establishment, of the very forces that deny justice to the Aborigines? Then, how thick was he with those powers, especially those that caused my downfall? These are the things which you must examine in your narrative, and not only examine, but come to conclusions about. A question should be: was it really my fault that I was so soundly defeated? You murmur about the ineptitude of my campaign, and I shout about a plot, a plot! Yes, a plot and he was part of that plot. Can you deny it? Listen, mate, I knew the ways of the Queensland Police Force at that time, and no matter whether a policeman was black or white or brindle, he was still part of the whole rotten set-up. He came out all right, didn't he, didn't he? Just like all the others, and next we'll find him a knight too. Sir Jacky of the Tribe of Judas.

'What, you want me to get to what you're paying me for? Am I boring you, mate? Too tedious for you, or is it truths striking home, eh? Listen, if you had been through the things I have, you wouldn't be so smug. Don't worry about the tape. It is on. A truth detector, isn't it? Well, I've finished with that farce of an election and at the part where the PM is about to offer me a job. I am to see him in three days' time and so I go to the scene of some of my greatest coups in real estate, not to work, but to relax in a resort there. In fact, and this again is in the strictest confidence . . . No, keep the tape on. It's all relevant, relevant!

'I did come out of the election with a little spare cash, not enough to pay off my debts, but enough for a few months in Surfers'. Well, enough of that. I was happily ensconced in the Xanadu Resort when I ran into an old acquaintance who invited me to a select party at the home of one of Queensland's most prominent socialites. On the spur of the moment I decided to attend. Why? Depression, the absence of a hangover, the need to seek diversion? It definitely wasn't with the object of meeting a woman, for Lady George only invited the ugliest and oldest and richest of the females who had made the Coast their burying ground. Her imagination did not descend to the demi-monde, or even to single women. So why did I decide to go? My anger at the PM had for the moment died down. I felt disgust at myself, at others and with everything. On the trucked-in clean sand of the artificial beach at Xanadu, I sank into a torpor and let the sun daze me into apathy while I waited for rain to match my mood. To think that once I had made a large killing from part of the land on which the resort sweltered. Now I actually smelt the corruption of the deals from the oil smeared over the naked breasts of the female bathers. Such beauty could be bought by a glance, or a word of admiration from the right sort of bloke. The wrong sort had to use money, fame or power and now I possessed precious little of these.

'I admit it, mate, all I had going for me was that tenuous connection with the PM. I was desperate, get me! And so I used the sun, the smooth water and the pure, well-swept sand to dull my mind. Sometimes I thought about my old school chum luxuriating in his sense of triumph. This too had been an old stamping ground of his and in fact he still retained a financial interest in the resort. Well, he had promised, but had he raised my hopes only to prepare to dash them? It was difficult to see why he would go in to bat for me. After all he was a political animal, and now in the heady rush of electoral victory coupled with the final declaration of Brisbane as the legal federal capital of Australia, he could let everything slide for a year or so. Then, I knew that my old school chum might find it extremely difficult to procure me an official, remunerative position in the higher echelons of the government service where I could recoup my fortune as well as pay off my creditors. It was difficult to imagine this after my electoral debacle; but for a moment, a long minute, I lay back on that pure sand imagining myself as the head of a committee inquiring into some such thing as organised crime. I had a huge salary, not too tedious work, the advantage of furthering my contacts in the course of the investigations, and frequent adjournments to attend to any little hobbies I might care to cultivate discreetly. Then, even in that humid heat, reality like a tropic downpour flooded me. I could not see myself enjoying that position for long. It was inevitable that my enemies would' begin their work of innuendo and insinuation, or if not that, I might be caught with my hand in the till, or be called to account over an outrageously padded expense account. And then, I knew this for certain, any hint of my being recommended for a position as chairperson of any committee of inquiry would arouse a storm of protests from the Opposition in the name of public accountability, virtue and the Australian way of keeping things in cupboards. I had been found out once too often. Questions would have been asked in the house, insults traded, files leaked and my name would have had to be hastily withdrawn. My old school chum would have been hard put to offer me anything more than a miserable consultative job which would have hardly paid enough to keep my creditors at bay. I would have been fobbed off with a pittance. Well, so much for the strength of the old school tie!

'And so, have I made myself clear on why I, I decided to attend that social do! In the hope that I might meet someone. Someone I could use in my efforts to bring about the downfall of my old school chum, or failing that, a politician or business-man I might use to retrieve my fortunes. I needed to find hope. I needed to regain my nerve. I had to find the courage to begin anew. I was at sixes and sevens. My soul was a tangled knot which I had to untie.

'As luck, or misfortune would have it, the Prime Minister was in attendance at the party, or rather the party danced attendance on him. He was the hero of the hour, though already daggers were being thrust into his back by those southerners who resented the rise of Queensland. I sought to establish contacts with a prominent enemy of his, but was rebuffed. Then during the evening when the spotlight had temporarily left the PM to focus in on a famous opera singer with the face of a horse who gargled "Queensland The Ultimate", he took the opportunity to draw me into the library which was shrouded in a gloom as dense as the gloom covering my mind. The only light was a reading lamp bent over a desk. He sat on the sofa to the left side of this light, sucked at his trademark pipe, extended his legs, bit down hard on the pipe stem, dragged it from his mouth between his thumb and forefinger, then spoke with all the gravity of the statesman which two consecutive electoral successes had supposedly made him.

' He stated: "Since yesterday, I have been carefully consider-ing your case with a number of close colleagues." He nodded his head to underline *colleagues*, then lifted his pipe, sucked on the stem, then lowered it again. Morosely, I watched this exercise in public relations, for in deference to the growing indignation of the anti-tobacco lobby, he never filled the pipe.

' "Yes," he continued, "we considered all aspects of your position." Again a pause, and although it was hard to pierce

21

the gloom, I was sure that his eyes were staring into mine in an attempt to wear away my incredulity. "I can see," he said, "that you don't exactly trust me, that you think that I am out to dupe you, or fob you off as quickly and as painlessly as possible. I assure you I have no intention of doing this." His hand went to his tie as if to emphasise an eternal boyhood connection.

' "Well, I have had some doubts, but I accept your bona fides. What have you got for me?" I asked, trying to hide my excitement. My old mate had come through.

'His teeth glimmered through the murk as he smiled what must have been his best media smile. I remember that the sharks were bad along the coast that year. "Ah, I see that we understand one another. Now listen carefully. After considering your position and your somewhat unique qualifications we have decided, in your best interests understand, that you should make yourself scarce for a while. Get away out of the country and out of the public eye."

'He paused to suck at his pipe. It was my turn to smile. I was, I was being offered an ambassadorship. I hoped that it was London. I knew that, as yet, I was not experienced enough for Tokyo or Washington; but, well, if not London, perhaps Paris, arrh . . . then!

' "We think that this is best after that election fiasco. It appears that you antagonised certain powerful interests who are about to administer the *public purse*. It is absolutely necessary that you get away, and so, well, there is this diplomatic post, newly created of course, which will be ideal for you. Of course, it is not in one of the more desirable countries, or even a nation in its own right as yet; but it is vitally important that Australia has some sort of representation there, not officially you understand, but someone to be on hand if things go awry. You see, your election campaign was not entirely a fiasco, for you did manage to get the black vote out. You have an aptitude in that direction as well as the necessary experience. Detective Watson Holmes Jackamara spoke highly of you. Just think if you had won that election, what with your black connection. Sorry, a jest; but this too is along those lines. You have become an expert on, shall we say, native peoples."

'I opened my mouth to say something, but he waved it shut.

' "Jackamara and I have been associates for some time. He is a man above average, and I am not one to let talent go unused . . . or unrewarded."

'There, there, these were his very words. Does it not show that Jackamara and that old rogue were in cahoots? During that reign of corruption he was hand in glove with them. What, don't you think so? Well, if you are honest, you'll expose that man for what he was, and possibly still is. Investigate him and you'll find that he was a traitor to your people. Let me ask you. Have you ever seen him march in a demonstration? Have you ever seen him come out in opposition to policies against the Aboriginal people? The answer is "no"! And you still want me to continue? . . . I shall and will. But first, isn't the tape running out? Best change it . . . I want all of this down . . . There, now where was I?

'After the, the PM made this startling disclosure, I tried to respond, but couldn't. To think that I was being offered a posting on the recommendation of my minder. It was too much, too too bloody much. How low the mighty have fallen, from the ultimate heights to the abysmal depths, and to think that I was the one who had first used that word ultimate to describe all things bright and Queensland.

' "It is an excellent posting, though, of course, there's no such thing as an embassy, or consulate; but let me assure you that the place is British, at least for the time being, and there'll be no problem with language."

' "Sweet Jesus," I exclaimed in a panic. "What have I done to deserve this? I'm being exiled, shipped off to some rotten, godforsaken place to rot. Do you take me for some kind of fool?"

' "You always were an excitable chap," the Prime Minister commented imperturbably. "Well, it may be a good thing in the place where you're going. Well, this country, or rather group of islands, is to achieve independence in the near future and the arrangements are now being drawn up in London in close consultation with our Department of Foreign Affairs. This island group after all is close to our shores, and we must not only have a say in its future, but must now learn about what's happening there: who are the local leaders, what's their political persuasion and so on and so forth. You'll be filled in on this in Canberra. So now you know the job. Only a fact-finding mission, you understand. Nothing else, but a fact-finding mission. You are not being forced into exile or any such absurdity like that. What I'm offering you is a cooling-off period away from your enemies. Look on it as a holiday, see it as a chance to get away and have time out to pull yourself together. God, how I envy you. Your own desert island, your own primeval South Sea island paradise. God, the opportunities there. A future Gold Coast and you there right at the beginning. It'll leave Surfers' for dead one day, and you have the savvy to make it happen to the advantage of yourself, Queensland and of course, Australia."

' "What, what?" I stuttered. This man was too, too much. They were getting rid of me on the cheap. Why had I threatened them?

' "I'd give my eyeteeth to be on the ground floor. Sad, sad, responsibilities of office and duty hold me in chains. So I offer this plum to you, old mate. It's yours, for the eating."

' "I'm the one who's being eaten," I muttered, feeling myself teetering on the edge of a great despair—the ultimate despair.

'He flung me a rope. "It could lead to much, much better things," he said, "that is if you wish to forsake commerce."

' "Such as?" I asked, jerking back from the edge.

' "An ambassadorship to Ireland and the Vatican, if you do the job well."

'Well, well that was more like it. My dear old school chum waited sucking on that wretched pipe. I thought of Ireland, the Emerald Isle and of warm Roman thighs. Why, I might become a papal knight. What did it matter if I was not a Catholic? Who would know? And that other place? It couldn't be that bad, and I'd be out of reach of my creditors. Before me stretched a gold brick road lined with opportunities and leading to the ultimate resort. The pot of gold glimmered at the end of the rainbow and I felt my hand trembling and my fingers clutching, seizing . . . A voyage to a far-off land, a South Sea island just waiting to be developed. But, but, I could never trust the old rogue. Where was the catch, where was it? Oh that I had known something about such islands and their ways . . .

'The Prime Minister stirred. He had given me enough rope to hang myself. He coughed into my silence and stated: "If this job isn't suitable, there's another one going which might help you out with your creditors. It's with the newly formed Company Police Squad. With your knowledge you should go far. What do you say to that?"

'I stood on the pivot of the seesaw. One end went down, then the other. I shifted my weight and evened them up. Policeman balanced against, well against diplomat. There was no choice and I knew it. I shifted off the pivot and the post of diplomat landed with a thud on the earth. "The Department of Foreign Affairs," I cried. "I shall be accredited of course."

' "Not at once," he replied. "It's rather hush-hush. It might be better that you be nominally under the secret service blokes for the period; but I promise you that you'll have a free hand, a diplomat's salary commensurate with your status and a liberal expense account."

' "Well, I'll just have to see how it goes," I said, refusing to let him see my eagerness . . .'

'Unfortunately, the PM took this as final. Things moved swiftly after that. Next morning, I was surprised to find a car waiting to whisk me to the airport where I was put on a plane to Canberra. There, I was enrolled in ASIO, given a code number, and taken to a training institute where I learnt to operate a radio transmitter and hand weapons. All this occurred over the next week. At the end of this period, I was offered a revolver which I took and stashed in my suitcase as I wasn't prepared to play the secret service wallah for anyone. Sufficient, even generous funds were placed at my disposal. I made sure that my salary was to be paid directly into my bank account which would make my bank manager more accommodating when my credit card account came due. It was strange and indeed out of character when the Prime Minister came to see me before the official swearing in. "See, mate, I'm really looking after you," he smiled that smile of his which never reached his wary eyes. Unconsciously, he reached into his pocket and pulled out his old pipe. He sucked on it as he regarded me. "Us Queenslanders stick together," he stated as if it was still the good old days. Then he added (and it was the reason why he had come to see me), "Of course, there is the formality of an oath to be taken under the Official Secrets Act, just a formality I assure you. You are really not part of ASIO, and have been seconded to my office, so that," and he smiled that smile of his, "so that, I can keep an eye out for you. Your mission will take about six months and your reports will be passed directly to me. In this way," and I swear he winked, "any little discrepancies will be safely ignored."

'After this I was taken to the office of the head of ASIO and the PM watched as I was sworn to secrecy forever and warned that any disclosure of government secrets would end in a long prison term. Then he quickly shook my hand and left me to stew in the knowledge that I had been duped again. If I now sought to disclose any information about him and his dealings, I would find myself up on a charge of treason before a secret court. I was still fuming as I rushed to the airport. But I was off on a Pacific paradise holiday. I wanted to meet a banker with development funds. Money was romance enough for me. That, at least, was what I thought as I embarked. Oh, that it had been so . . . '

SESSION THREE

'So you see, I was a constant victim of political chicaneries which pushed me from pillar to post. Perhaps I should have hesitated; but I was in the grip of forces which kept me off balance, and these forces were being manipulated not only by the PM, but by Jackamara too. I'm almost sure of this, and if there was any justice in the world, a Royal Commission should have been convened to investigate these matters. The oath of secrecy has bound me all these years and it is only now that I dare speak out. I see you smile again, as if you think I am a victim of my own paranoia. Well, think that, and as for your man, Jackamara, I am not libelling him, God forbid, but I believe that he did have a hand in knitting the net of deceit and trickery in which I became entangled. Whether you believe it or not, you as a, more or less, impartial investigator may form your own conclusions, but beware, beware . . . the forces arrayed against us are powerful, extremely powerful, too powerful to buck without . . . Oh, forget it. You are less than I am; you will never become as much as I have been. No one is interested in you and, and, perhaps, not even in me now. A lowly clerk without any political pull at all, chained to his desk by the Official Secrets Act. To speak out is to become a criminal, but I have ceased caring. Then who would believe me . . . except my enemies?

'At the airport, I was ushered through with the minimum of fuss onto one of the smaller jets, a Boeing 727D or some such designation I believe it to have been. At the time I was less interested in my aircraft than in the sudden lightening of my mood. I felt I was at last escaping from the net of subterfuge in which I had been entangled since that accursed election, and moreover, I would be out of reach of my creditors. I became exultant. I was on an official mission, no matter how dubious a ploy it was to get me out of the way.

'The Prime Minister wasn't such a bad chap after all. He had come through for me after the chips were down. "Don't you worry about that." I muttered this famous Queenslander expression as a hostess personally escorted me to my first-class seat, rushed off for the latest *Business Weekly*, then returned to do up my seat belt. I was sitting in an aisle seat and what was more beside a striking woman with red hair who, when she glanced at me, had the greenest eyes flecked with gold. Her skin was golden too, hinting at the tropics and the South Sea paradise to which I was allegedly bound. As the rich aroma of her perfume filled my nostrils, I could not help but think: "My dear, you are just right for me. My kind of development." Yes, yes, I know, I was foolish to think that my past was safely behind me and that at last my luck had changed; but I thought so then. I checked the share market in that magazine. I noted that my little flutter was fluttering upwards and would necessitate a fax to my stockbroker. Yes, I was on the rise again.

'Thus I was perfectly in the right to be elated, and if I had then been capable of the slightest poetic description, I might have jotted down a poem on the miracle sitting beside me; but then I had no such gift. The so-called beauties of nature passed me by. I considered such things as aspects of real estate which might go to inflate the prices of hillside properties. "Such a barren soul," you might exclaim, and with good reason; but all this would change with the coming of love into my life. Poetry and the gift of verse would follow. I wonder if that Jackamara of yours has a poetic soul, for his story certainly stuck in my mind—is that the attribute of a good storyteller?— and it stuck to me. In fact, eventually, I would feel myself becoming such a creature, a *Kwinkan*, a spirit-stick of nature without the supernatural powers to change myself. In fact I would be imprisoned within this persona and I would find myself regretting the loss of my humanity though filled with exaltation as I wallowed in the romantic suffering of it all. But all this came later, much later. Now I was still the crass entrepreneur, content in myself as the engines rose into a whining scream which flung us off the earth and straight through the air until in a matter of minutes we were over the splendid harbour of Sydney. There below hunched the bridge, beside it the dazzling white sails of the Opera House and the blue waves of the Pacific curling in a froth of, of sperm against the land. The coast fled behind me, and I was thinking that I needed a drink to relax my nerves. Flying raises anxiety in me. I need the clefts and crevasses of, of well, of a city about me. Surrounded by masses of man-made rock, I am at home and can hide away from all that I feel I must hide away from; but, but, I drag the world in after me, and my misery is exposed on a stage for all to see. Gloomy, aren't I? I force a smile up from the ultimate depths. Sir, I was the brightest spark on the Gold Coast. What functions I held. I burnt the candle at both ends and blazed from dusk to dawn, while my companies languished, my debts grew and the vultures gathered. Enough, enough, I digress . . .

'As the plane lurched a little as it crossed the edge of the continental shelf, I sipped on my whisky and soda. As it threaded its way through huge white clouds, I finished my drink and relaxed in the mellow glow of the alcohol. I rubbed my hands together as I contemplated how my luck had changed. "Yeah, yes," I whispered, as the plane entered the pass between the serrated peaks of a high cloud mass. It was then that I offered the beautiful woman at my side a drink. Not only did she accept, but drew my attention to her companion. I did a double take, for it was Miss Riyoko Tamada, the manageress of The Hitaka Resort on the Spit. She was considered to be an astute businesswoman, though I could not verify this as unfortunately I had been repulsed when I tried to inveigle my way in to see her. From all accounts, not only was she in charge of the resort, but she had a pipeline to the directors of the giant Kitsune Corporation which had unlimited funds at its disposal. Well, well, she was a find, and in other circumstances I would have ignored the other woman and concentrated on the Japanese, but I was drawn to that beauty in spite of the pot of gold sitting next to her. But then, I quickly learnt she too was a catch: the founder of the Smooth As Satin company whose well-known Sas Shops collected the loot in many major and minor cities across the world. I was in excellent and rich company, and female. I sat back to enjoy myself.

'As we sipped and conversed away the tedious hours, I felt myself coming under the spell of my beautiful seat mate. Thankfully, Miss Tamada kindly consented to bury her face in her personal computer, and by bury, I mean bury, for she kept her face almost on the screen so that it could not be seen by us. Still, it left the way clear for me to attempt to clinch the deal. Having had much practice in eliciting valuable information from gullible clients and not so gullible business associates, I quickly found out that she was 28, was a seasoned traveller who had seen most of the countries on the globe, was unmarried and belonged to a rich family which had plantations on the very group of islands to which I was proceeding. If I had not been feeling so, well, so high, I might have questioned this coincidence, but I knew that my luck had changed and this led to my lamentable lack of caution. In fact, I even failed to enquire why she was travelling with Miss Riyoko Tamada. I merely accepted her as a chance acquaintance. A moth to her butterfly, so to speak. As a businessman, ready to seize the first opportunity, this was a mistake. What excuse? I was dazzled by the beauty beside me. Why, even the PM had been known to fall. We're all mortals, mate, and when the old sap rises a pair of pretty eyes has more appeal than an unlimited expense account.

'As the aeroplane whined its way over the blue of the Pacific and Miss Tamada's personal computer now and again beeped, we became more and more intimate in our conversation, or at least she did. On the whole I managed to say very little. It was my motto to let the sucker blab and although I did not see her as a sucker, she did blab. Her name was Carla and she explained the German derivation by explaining that she, on her father's side, belonged to an old Hanseatic family which had arrived in England with George III, or some such number. She had just been in the UK. The registered headquarters of

Sas was on the Isle of Wight, though the nerve centre of operations was in London. Now she was on her way home, having had to detour through Australia as no airlink existed, as yet, between London and her group of islands. She did not mention her companion, and I did not ask why she was travelling with perhaps the most powerful woman on the Gold Coast. It was an omission I should have rectified, but I was infatuated with Carla. As we sipped on our sixth drink, she confided that more and more she found not only Britain, but also Australia stuffy with a stuffiness of the spirit which depressed her and made her hurry home. She shrugged as she said that it made her feel that her body was physically restricted as if by a girdle. "And the Lord knows I have no use for such a contraption," she added, laughing as she arched her back to show her perfect lines. I returned the laugh as I boldly admired her. Was it any wonder that I believed that my luck had changed? "Smooth as satin" indeed!

'I enjoyed her displays of femininity. I luxuriated in the aura of her shining red hair, in the golden light from her jade eyes, in the silver laughter from her full red lips. She was brimming over with well-being, joy and radiance. Was it any wonder that I fell under her spell? How could anyone, any man, not be taken in by her decisive manner, the freedom of her life, her way of talking randomly and slightly twisting meanings so that a bizarre shape emerged which hinted at things unsaid?

'It was then that I gained, or found, what I now consider to be my poetic soul. She called to mind the primeval freedom of virgin forests and the intensity of the burning tropics cooled by lagoons of sweet, sweet water. I imaged her as the Eve of the marvellous paradise to which I was bound, not as some sort of shady spy, but as a defender arriving to watch over the interests of her soon-to-be-independent nation. The desire arose to tie the fortunes and destinies of both our countries together. It was then that Miss Tamada called for another drink, pointed at something on the screen to Carla, then smiled and lightly caressed her arm. And it was then that I should have pulled back and queried why the representative of a major Japanese corporation was travelling with the woman, especially one who appeared on intimate terms with her. I didn't, not just then. Being besotted does not make for alertness in business. She flashed a smile at me and the lotus flowers of intoxication bloomed as I watched the play of her features and I wanted that hand on her arm to be my hand. How smooth her skin looked. I imagined her running naked along a wide, white beach as natural as her Sas models appeared in TV ads. Her company specialised only in the most rare and natural oils and unguents uniquely and purely prepared for the most extravagant of women, who strangely enough were imaged also as the most natural. When she squeezed past me to go to the toilet, I wanted to set her free of her restricting skirt which urged attention to her rounded buttocks. It was then that Miss Tamada turned her narrow eyes on me and wrinkled her tiny nose. "You are so and so", she said. "Once we were considering that piece of land you controlled on the Spit. Now it is ours." Her eyes then shifted from me to watch Carla returning to her seat. There was a covert form of hostility in her words, but I ignored them. After all she was not only a woman, but a very slight one, and at the moment I wasn't in the market for investment funds. "So up you, sister," I whispered loud enough for her to hear, then my eyes and attention switched to Carla.

'As we settled into what appeared to be a friendship far different from the casual acquaintanceship usually struck up on long flights, our conversation settled on our coming destination of Fiji and the next leg of our journey. I was surprised to learn that there was, as yet, no airport on the island. I had not been informed of this and I could not but wonder why. All my suspicions concerning the Prime Minister returned, and I could not help thinking that I, having become an embarrassment, had had to be rushed out of Oz on any pretext. I doubted if the powers that be would even care if I reached my designated station. In fact, it was only a convenient spot in the universe to steer me towards. My absence from Australia had been accomplished with little fuss and bother. Perhaps the PM in his wisdom, counted on my being in funds and rushing off to greener pastures, to America for example. I admit that the idea was pleasant. The Land of the Fast Buck and boundless opportunities beckoned; but what stopped me was that bloody oath and the piling of a further crime on top of my already high stack. It was unwise for me to skip out, especially when gazing into those green-golden-flecked eyes and that full, rich mouth which promised a sweetness of fresh strawberries. I lowered my gaze to those ivory fingers so tantalisingly long, moved a little up to that body swelling beneath the rich cloth, swelling with an urgency which called me to duty . . . and besides she was rich!

'As we replenished our glasses, I took her a little into my confidence and told her of my predicament: that I had no way at present of reaching my post. To cloak my mission, I had to invent an occupation. I had been idly flipping through the airline magazine and my eyes rested on an article. I found a profession. I became an embryologist on my way to the islands to study pelagic jelly, to hunt among gastropods, corals and what have you for the primordial cell of life, a tiny spot of slime reputed to linger on in the warm waters of that island chain.

'Carla received my series of measured lies as if they were the truth, or as if she understood what I was talking about. I hoped she hadn't read the article, as I absurdly and vainly embroidered the few lines I had read. I became a scientist of renown with a career of academic success which needed to be fleshed out by field-work. This voyage of mine, or rather flight, was to be the crown of my work, perhaps leading to the Nobel Prize. But, but I had to reach those islands, I had to embark on my researches as soon as possible. Why, it might, it should lead to the understanding of the origin of life on our planet. She listened to most of my words and I saw that at least she detected the passion beneath them. At last I paused to judge the result, and calmly she informed me that there was a vessel, a schooner called *Tui-tui* which sailed between Fiji and the islands regularly. This vessel would be waiting for her, and as the captain was a good friend, there was no doubt that he would find room for me.

We were such mates by now that I touched her arm as I thanked her. The Boeing swooped down to land at Nadi and she took the time to phone through to confirm our passages on the schooner which was sailing next morning. It was only natural that we were booked into the same hotel where I arranged to meet both women for dinner. I would have wished to have Carla for myself, but Miss Tamada clung to her and could not be excluded. As I showered in the air-conditioned coolness, I exulted at how things had worked out. Indeed, my luck had changed. Feeling absolutely refreshed I went down to the foyer to send one fax signalling that I had arrived and then another to my broker ordering him to sell my shares and to invest the proceeds in The Smooth As Satin Holding Company.

SESSION FOUR

'I suppose we all have our visions of South Sea island paradises. I thought about palm tress, banana trees, breadfruit trees, coconut trees—a plethora of trees—languid lagoons, white-wreathed islands, necklets of bright coral, swaying beautiful women eager to please. Ah, that old black magic of the colonial masters, or European sailors. See, I am not racist, nor am I that naive. Cynicism, my usual weapon for dealing with the world and its too many illusions, is a superior weapon often able to shoot down all fond dreams. But it is fragile, so fragile, one which easily runs out of ammunition, or spare parts. Once, and once only, let yourself believe in beauty and love all encircled by a South Sea island paradise, and the weapon shatters in your hands. Disarmed, I could only surrender to suffering . . . but let that be, I continue. The hotel was as any other hotel—we had better in Surfers'—but at least it was modern and was shut tight in air-conditioned coolness against the heat and smog of tatty Suva. In such confinement, seated at the bar or lazing about the enclosed pool, it was easy for me to dream about paradise, especially as I exchanged smiles with brown-skinned natives eager to satisfy most of my whims. At a price, it is true, for life there was every bit as hungry as a Queensland tycoon ready to clinch a deal with the latest Western Australian upstart. Yes, even there, human nature would not and could not be denied . . .

'Carla did not appear for breakfast, but Miss Tamada was there coolly informal in shirt and shorts. The dapper conservative businesswoman style had been dispensed with. Now I saw a doll who might even be fun; but she shot me an unpleasant glance, and I fell into confusion.

' "Ah, Miss Tamada, you are on holiday," I exclaimed, trying for a smile.

35

'She wrinkled her nose at me, and then sipped her coffee. I thought that she was going to ignore me, but then she said: "Suva is not very pleasant, but some of the resorts here are first class."

' "And you should know," I gently needled her, for the Kitsune Corporation owned more than several.

' "Of course, it is my business, but enough of business," and she smiled a smile as cold as that of the PM, then tugged at the side of her shirt which had slipped off her shoulder. She had nicely rounded flesh, and at other times I might have been greatly interested, for here was sitting not a woman, but a business opportunity, though Japanese corporations were impossible to break into. They kept all to themselves politely.

' "Do you like the ocean?" she asked me.

' "All Australians do," I replied visualising the built-up strip from Brisbane to Sydney where even the smallest lot was worth its weight in gold if it had a view of the ocean.

' "Not all, for I have a friend who loves the desert. I go and visit him sometimes. The desert is so dry and the sea is so wet. Yet, yet, I live beside the sea. Contradiction, no?" and she flashed her teeth at me. Little teeth which, were they to give one a nip, might bring blood.

'Then the atmosphere turned sweet with longing as Carla appeared sleeky beautiful in white slacks and blouse. She went to Miss Tamada, ran her fingers over her bare arm, then sat down beside her. I remained standing, for I had arisen as soon as she had entered. Now both women stared up at me, and suddenly I felt ridiculous in my stubby shorts and casual shirt, long white socks and sturdy shoes. It did not help matters that the women looked at one another, then again at me. I felt as out of place as I would have in one of the Sas shops.

' "Please, won't you sit and finish your breakfast," Carla said.

' "A praying mantis," spluttered the Japanese woman into her coffee.

'She went down in my estimation at once. It was no way for a businesswoman to behave, or for one to dress for that matter. Carla next to her appeared so much more sophisticated.

'We managed to get through the meal with the minimum amount of conversation. My whole day had been spoilt. Then it was time to leave our air-conditioned haven for the heat of the streets. Our gear was loaded into a taxi. The morning was heating up to a livid noon, as we struggled through streets blue with exhaust fumes. I dripped with sweat, the final fat of my good days melting away. I felt miserable, though I was used to the heat and should have taken it in my stride, or as perfectly as the two women who had scarcely a damp patch on them. Miss Tamada, to add to my misery, began rattling away to Carla about how the warmth made her feel as dry as a dead leaf. I heard Carla reply about how when she perspired it felt as if her soul was leaking out to fill the universe. This was a direct steal from me. The previous night at dinner, in my academic persona, I had made some inane remark about how sometimes we felt that our souls permeated the world, and Carla had eaten the proposition with avidity. To make matters worse, Carla mentioned that her Sas shops now had a line in male toiletries. This seemingly innocent remark elicited a titter from Miss Tamada and a scowl from me. I asked the taxi driver to stop and got in beside him. I had had enough of female company for the time being.

'The taxi crawled to the harbour and died on the wharf beside our so-called schooner. Carla remarked to Miss Tamada that her family owned the boat, and it was through such remarks that I learnt that her family had a monopoly on inter-island transport, and that with Independence looming in the near future, they were, in conjunction with Kitsune, developing an international airport for the emerging nation. I could understand that, as well as the need for taking aboard a Japanese partner with unlimited funds. Yes, I had done the same thing in my wheeling and dealing along the Gold Coast, though there I had been in competition with others. Here, it appeared that Carla's family had a monopoly, or more likely a stranglehold on the economic life of the island chain, and that with independence this would continue without hindrance, though I remembered that there was an Opposition of a sorts, which might bode well for me, for if the family control could be broken, then there was room for an astute businessman to get in on the ground floor. I had to keep my ears open for the main opportunity, and being almost an accredited representative of the Australian Government would help me to extend the foot in the door to the whole leg, then Bob's your uncle and I would be in. My mood lifted as I contemplated my profitable future and even if I failed to do a deal with the Opposition there was still Sas and Kitsune available. I felt so good that I smiled at my female companions. Yes, I could indeed establish a profitable partnership with them.

'Most women, though I am not being sexist (these days no businessman can afford to be) have the gift of the gab, and my beauteous Carla was no exception. As our luggage was being loaded, she told me that a few years ago a minor tourist boom had startled Fiji (and most of the Pacific) after a remake of the film *Mutiny on the Bounty*, and the schooner had rocked on the swell and hastily been converted into the present craft which mocked the sleekness the word "schooner" conjured up. Masts and sails remained, but only for effect. The canvas rotted on the cross-trees and the two stubby masts were like the stumps on a hastily cleared block of land. A second tier of cabins had been built on the deck and these made the vessel resemble an old Sydney ferry. I stared at the top-heavy boat and inwardly shuddered. I guessed that a sea of any size might capsize the thing in a minute.

'I mentioned this to Miss Tamada, who wrinkled her nose at me. This was a mannerism which I was beginning to find most annoying. Now she opened her computer and busily entered some figures. She tapped once, twice, three times, then closed the lid. "Yes, it is not nice, but it will be scrapped soon." And that was that, or was it, for the captain heard her words and scowled. I looked at him. In the sleek rush of progress about to engulf the soon-to-be-independent nation, he would be as out of place as his boat.

'He was a hulking, heavy-moustached, red-faced Pommy who had been washed ashore by the colonial tide which then receded leaving him high and dry and all at sea. He greeted Carla with a few pleased grunts, ignored me and Miss Tamada, then shouted at his "boys" as he called the native men of his crew, to gently handle the luggage. We were the only passengers and were given two of the top cabins, one for me and the other for the two women. Carla informed me that they were cooler than those below decks. This may have been true, but I entered a furnace and instantly sought relief in the main dining-cum-lounge-cum-saloon where fans pushed air over my saturated body.

'Carla came in to urge me to go on deck to see the *Tui-tui* leave harbour. "There'll be a breeze of sorts," she said with a laugh directed at my flushed face and dripping forehead. I snarled at her dry skin as I followed her onto the upper deck and into the glaring heat of the tropic sun. Miss Tamada was already sitting beneath a patch of canvas, with a small hand fan fluttering languidly. I sagged beside her, as I heard a rumble and felt the deck tremble under my feet. Half-naked brown bodies untied the vessel and soon she was chugging out from a harbour which had less attraction than the remains of the Brisbane docks at midsummer. I sat limply under the sun which symbolised the heavy burden of my present as my lungs gasped pulling in the heated air, then convulsed and flung it out. How I longed for Surfers' and the cool air-conditioned bars in which formerly I had conducted much of my business. With a muttered excuse to the women, I retreated to the lounge, saloon or what have you to find that an air-conditioning unit had purred into action. At last! I relaxed and felt my mood lightening as I opened a fridge to find it stacked with Powers beer. I cracked a cool one and toasted modern technology which had made it possible for the white man not only to live in the tropics but to turn them to a pretty profit. Only in the late afternoon did I, somewhat befuddled, return to the deck to catch a last glimpse of Fiji.

'It was a dark smudge astern. Above and around and below

was nothing but the blue of the sky merging into the blue of the ocean. The heat sent me reeling back to the saloon, to find Carla and Miss Tamada bent over the computer. They snapped it off as I entered and Carla cool and regal in a halter-neck top and knee-length shorts went to the refrigerator to get me a cold beer. She and her companion settled for mineral water. Well, that was all right with me, for it left more of the amber fluid for my good self, and if the heat continued I would need every drop. I sucked on my can and remarked on the blue of the sea and sky. The remark passed without comment, and then Miss Tamada, in her snide way, asked me how my business interests were going. I replied that this had only been a hobby to fund my research and that now I was attached to Bond University. She wrinkled her nose at this and I felt my mood falling. I brightened up as I met Carla's smile. I began a probing conversation with her about the resources of the island chain to which we were bound. Miss Tamada smirked as Carla remarked that as I did not seem to have brought diving equipment along for my search for pelagic jelly, I might borrow hers when we reached the island. I nodded and towards evening, we made our way onto the deck to enjoy the stiff breeze, or trade wind which was blowing. I sat next to Carla and experienced the Pacific Ocean in all its travel poster glory. All would have been perfect if Carla had unveiled her body in the skimpiest of bikinis. Ah, but that was not to be. Still, I felt resurrected and laughed and joked with Carla as I snuffed up the air in delighted gulps. To add to my elation, Miss Tamada left and I had Carla to myself.

'How wonderful everything was. The air held the odour of a fur which has just fallen from the shoulders of a beautiful woman. This, I knew, was the fabled perfume of the tropics. And since the sun had set, the sea and sky no longer dazzled, but shone gently with the subtle hues of paradise. The sky as translucent as the ceiling of the foyer of Jupiter's Casino, was a golden green streaked with the pink gleams of that subdued chandelier termed the sun. The atmosphere felt like the atmosphere of the special room for high rollers and the sea pulsated with the tasteful music of a not too energetic dance number especially rendered for the rich and famous. It stretched away from us like the transparent floor of a disco illuminated with rippling wave notes. At ease and clutching my tinny, I sat next to my beautiful, red-headed companion, feeling and almost believing that I was one of those handsome males in a Sas, or better still, a beer advertisement, who glance across to find love as a slim hand gracefully offers them a cold Powers as a token of that love. It really was like that, just then, for I need not say, although I do, do say it that Carla attracted me the way rotten meat attracts blowies. I'm sorry, perhaps the image is not only inappropriate, but inept. I'll try again, as, as, well, as your tape-recorder attracts my words. There, it was as self-evident as that . . . The captain for all his dourness—he was a Scot by the way and hated the English—was charmed, and even the native crew stormed the racial barrier, though it might have been that they recognised part of themselves in this regal woman who was descended from the chiefs of the island chain. They went out of their way to please her and saw to it that all her wants were satisfied. Carla accepted this adulation with aloofness, and even gently mocked the captain who was not your canny Scot of legend, but a thick-headed, less than amusing oaf with an absurdly British sense of superiority and absence of tact which rested calmly along with his racism.

'Perhaps, I should have, should have kept a journal to detail what I felt on that voyage. I didn't and have only memories and even these are fragmented. Once, the night was soft velvet and the prow of our vessel parted the silken sea as gently, as gently as a lover parts the thighs of his beloved. The thud thud of the motor continued on evenly like languid heartbeats, and then, there began an absurd conversation on shipwrecks and Carla gaily quoted from the poem "The Ancient Mariner", and laughed at the skipper who did flash a "glittering" eye. This evil eye made forays over her body. It wandered over the length of her bare legs, stopped briefly at the vee of her shorts, climbed to the twin curves of flesh pressing out her halter-neck top, and drifted up to her throat, her lips, her nose, her eyes, her forehead and tumbled down her hair. The atmosphere became charged with the musk of his lust. Then Miss Tamada whispered in her ear, and Carla smiled and directed a question at the red-eyed lout: "Have you really eaten human flesh?"

'The captain positively looked embarrassed, then glanced at me before replying: "Can't say that I have, but I ken them that has."

' "And what would the taste be like? Did those, those friends of yours tell you?" she asked, letting a slight tone of disgust tinge her voice. The oaf stared at the dark waters and playing the old sea-dog, sniffed the salty air.

' "Was it delicious? Riyoko here has a taste for things exotic, and just this morning she was detailing to me the preparation of Fuju. She is absolutely delighted to find that our waters abound in puffer fish. I'm dying to try it," . . . and she gave a delicious shiver.

'Miss Tamada smiled a smile better suited to the boardroom rather than to the deck of a schooner. All that she needed to accomplish the stereotype of a businesswoman was glasses and perhaps a statuesque body. The lean and hungry look really goes down well in business circles.

' "Well, she is waiting." And I do believe that that absolute doll of a woman licked her lips, before continuing to bait the skipper. "She has heard the story that in Fiji the people, in order to terrify the Indians who were gaining dominance, once dug a long trench which they declared to be an earth oven and in which they were intending to cook them. But oddly, they are all good Christians now and have put such cannibalistic things behind them. Still, Christians do consume the body and blood of Jesus and perhaps they were ready to serve up baked Indian."

'The captain was ill at ease. His "glittering" eye was no more and his face was wan. He made a gesture of protest before answering in an exaggerated accent which made a mockery of his words: "Well, you ken lassie, they call it long pig out here. The heathens used to eat it as we eat mutton or beef. Some of 'em's still got the taste for it. Just think, how succulent young pork is. How it melts in the mouth . . . "

' "Yes, yes, I believe I can taste it," Carla whispered, seeming to lose her composure over such a perversion. "I expect that they preferred some races . . . " she added, adopting the same half-taunting tone as the captain, smiling at Miss Tamada before continuing, "such as the Indian. I don't know about Japanese; but then I know there is eating and eating," and she smiled again at her companion. Their eyes locked for a moment, then both stared at the old seadog.

' " 'Tis so, Lassie, 'tis so. For starters, there's your Chinaman," he hesitated and looked at Miss Tamada whose eyes had turned feral. Bravely he went on: "His grub's soya sauce, ginger and suchlike things that gets into the flesh and gives it a fragrance prized above all in New Guinea, but among these islands they preferred the Paki above the Chinee. A rare treat your Paki was. All those curries and spices give a tartness to the flesh—at least they say so," and he broke off, suddenly flushing a deep, rich red.

' "And what about Europeans such as yourself?" Carla asked with a half smile directed at Miss Tamada.

' "Lassie, lassie . . . " the captain protested.

' "It is a well-known fact that when their food supply gives out Europeans like a slice of, of long pig," she replied tartly. "I have heard that they develop a craving for it."

' "Too true, too true, and they who develops a taste for it, can't stop 'emselves," the captain whispered . . .

'The culinary conversation was beginning to nauseate me. I was about ready to leave the group when Miss Tamada said quietly: "But there is flesh and flesh. Japanese would never eat dead human flesh, though some might like it fresh just like some like to eat monkey brains directly from the skull of the living animal. Perhaps it is possible to develop a taste for such things, just as I have developed a taste for business. It happened quite a while ago now. When I was a child I enjoyed exploring empty lots with off-limit signs. In them I imagined I would find rotten corpses, but all I found were different kinds of insects. Still, it was a delicious feeling, a scary feeling as I searched into every corner of a lot. I used to feel that the place was all mine and that something terrifying or marvellous might happen there. I had the most crazy fantasies as I roamed around. Among the wildly growing grass, I would see a scene of murder, a naked man and woman, the ghosts of a woman or child, but never, never the sight of humans cooking up a nice dish of long pig. I leave such fantasies to our captain. We have other ones . . . " She looked directly at Carla who moved next to her and took her hand as she continued: "When I was much older, I had a friend, Kumi. She knew of a lot that was desolate and deserted. She said that it was very large with a big muddy pond with some fish in it. Naturally I wanted to go there, for she said that that every time she went to that place, she had the vague urge to kill someone. Not that she had a particular individual in mind, but she wanted to come across some one there and hit him or her with a rock. She even had decided to throw the body into the pond. She wanted to see that body rot, and watch what the water did to it . . . "

'This perhaps was worse than the captain meandering on about human flesh, and it was infinitely more perverted to hear it from the rosebud lips of that tiny Japanese woman. Carla caressed her as she continued on in her low voice: "She brought up that scary kids' feeling in me and I wanted to go there. It was then Kumi said: 'But I can't promise that I won't kill you there.' This added to the thrill as I laughed and said: 'Then, I'll come back as a ghost.' We were walking along at the time and I went along with her and stayed at her place until suppertime. She had a little girl, Nana, and as we talked she constantly interrupted us. 'Say', Kumi said once, 'I'm sure that you don't remember this, but once you told me that you wouldn't mind if I killed you. Do you really mean it? Will you let me kill you?' It was then that Nana wanted to pee. We took her and watched."

'Something was going on between the two women. Carla's hand had stopped stroking Miss Tamada's arm. Now, it gripped and I swear that I saw bruises start up beneath her fingers. Miss Tamada continued: " 'Of course not,' I replied, pretending that Kumi was joking. It was then that Nana finished and made a face. We both burst out laughing. Kumi took her daughter on her lap, then declared to my face: 'You were scared. I couldn't seriously talk about dying, killing and things like that. You should be ashamed of yourself.' I was embarrassed, and then she began to attack me. 'You're disgusting and sneaky. It gets to me. But you are my pet, my little pet fox. Hey, look at me. Don't be nervous.' "

' "As I turned my face to Kumi, she grabbed my hair and pulled it. I tried to pull away, but now both my neck and wrist were in her hands. I gave up, then Kumi began to shake my body in a wild motion, her eyes wide open. Nana was between us. The girl thought we were playing some sort of game and started to giggle. I gave in to Kumi. After a time, she loosened her grip and sighed: 'That's right, what is important is a certificate.' I knew then that she envied me my, my qualifications. I stroked her face, looking at her lips which were cracked. Dark red blood was oozing out. Some of the lipstick had rubbed off and she looked a fright. Then a few tears appeared in the corner of her eyes. At that moment, Nana jumped at Kumi and she fell onto the floor. She climbed up on Kumi, grabbed her hair, and pretended she was riding a horse. She kicked her mother's chest, yelling: 'Giddy-up, horsie, giddy up.' I heard Kumi moan and I grabbed Nana's arm and pulled her off. She bit my hand and I kicked her. She cried loudly as children do when they are shocked more than hurt. It was enough for me to put my hands over my ears to block out the cries."

' "Kumi smiled at me and tried to pull herself up by holding onto my ankles. She did this suddenly and I fell face down, on top of her as if I was embracing her. Neither of us moved for awhile. I felt the heavy beating of her heart on my body. I stroked her hair. She was still. I closed my eyes while I continued to stroke. Soon I heard her regular breathing and then I bent down and tasted the blood on her lips. I lapped it up and it was so sweet, so sweet this taste of the wine of her body. And that was my first taste of blood, my very first taste."

'Miss Tamada stopped and we men looked embarrassed, and then Carla asked: "And that vacant lot, did you ever see it?"

' "I did and it was my first development for Kitsune. Now it is an apartment building and I have an apartment in it. Somehow when I am there, I remember Kumi. I feel so close to her, so close to that first taste."

'I seized the opportunity to go off for a cold beer, then returned to the deck but instead of going back to the group, I went aft to stare down into our wake. I was leaning there when something whizzed by with a scream, just missing me and plopped into the water. It was the ship's cat and someone had flung it deliberately at me. If it had landed, I might have been a mess of scratches, or worse, in fending it off I might have fallen overboard, and so goodbye to me. Shaken, I stared at the dark spot which I imagined was the cat. I felt nothing for it. It was an awful scabby creature which befriended no one. I wondered who had used it as an instrument of attack, and whether it was a cruel joke. Then I remembered the revolver in my suitcase. Instantly, I went to my cabin to check it out. It was too bulky to conceal on my person. I shrugged and left it there. I finished my beer, got another one, and decided that the whole thing must have been a joke, or if not that the demented animal had launched itself at me. Thus quieting my fears, I went back to the group who appeared to have noticed nothing. The topic of conversation had changed to the merits and demerits of colonialism.

'Carla attempted to distance herself from the colonisers. "So you had to carve out those territories, did you?" she flung at the captain.

' "Lassie, lassie, your great-grandfather was one of the best carvers in these parts. Was for their own good—got to be civilised, you ken."

' "So to civilise them we established our plantations and forced them to work in them. If they died out, we imported Indians to do the work. So we stopped them eating each other, or dying from starvation in India, by turning them into slaves. We became the cannibals, not of their bodies, but of their souls. Now, after we've removed much of the native and hopefully replaced it with the slave, we are intending to give them independence while holding onto the assets and power."

' "Or sharing it with us," remarked Miss Tamada. "The masters and mistresses lack capital and that is where we come in. We Japanese have never been colonised nor have we been colonisers. We are not part of that world."

' "But what about Korea and Manchuria?" I couldn't help butting in, remembering the Korean businessman I had had some dealings with and his opinion of the Japanese occupation of his country.

' "Well, what about them and your New Guinea? Our little foray ended in our soldiers eating human flesh. Now we can't even remember those times. Once we marched out to conquer, now we wait and they, you all come to us."

' "Oh doll, oh doll," exclaimed Carla, suddenly getting up and moving away.

' "When we lost India, we lost everything," the captain broke in, in a drunken voice with a sob tearing up from his imperial soul.

' "Wet, wet," exclaimed Miss Tamada, following Carla who leant over the railing. They huddled together and the conversation came to an end. I gulped my beer and the captain sipped his whisky.

'The night grew old in dazzling splendour. Around us the sea flamed and great stretches of phosphorescent fire flowed. In the dark patches between, I imagined the naked bodies of Carla and Miss Tamada embracing as mother and child in the midst of despoiled and cannabalised bodies. I became maudlin and longed to have Carla for myself. We Europeans had grown old and tired and needed new blood to bring us energy. What use were we, when we lacked the vision to complete ourselves in this paradise? The captain and myself were far from home, whereas this was where Carla belonged and she was in the process of discarding that part which was her European heritage for another which was stronger and more, more potent. Yet, yet, I had vision and enough nous to carve out my own plantations. I would do it with Carla. I would, I would, and then for the first time I heard a sniggering within me which I instinctively knew came from that *Kwinkan* soul of mine. I hung over the water and in the crevasses between the waves, siren shapes formed to beckon me. Then I shuddered as I saw caught at the end of a trailing rope, the body of that wretched cat. Caught by the neck, it bobbed and thrust against the side of the boat. I vomited and bile came to embitter my lips. I found the rope and untied the end. The cat flung itself away and was gone. How I wish that I had floated away with it, for the conversation had upset me more than I could admit, then . . . '

SESSION FIVE

'Perhaps with my last words you may think that I was falling into that mood of despondency which, I have heard, often befalls Europeans in the tropics. This definitely was not so. I enjoyed delightful company, had a plentiful supply of my favourite Queensland beer, the heat had lessened to an agreeable warmth and I was embarked on a five-day voyage to a chain of unspoilt islands. Any tourist would have given his eyeteeth to be in my shoes . . . But, why do you mention that cat, that mangy animal which had succumbed to mania and launched itself at me? Cats are like that and the boat was better off without it. No, nothing else happened to me. I tell you I was in an enjoyable, in fact a blissful position which you are right to envy. I ask you, have you sailed along in your own enchanted world alone with the boundless ocean and sky . . . and perhaps a cannibal skipper? Come on, they were having me on. And the Japanese woman and her dislike? A very successful businesswoman of the Kitsune Corporation who was attractive in her own petite way. Those oriental women . . . you get me? No, I am not being sexist, I give her her due.

'Well, the day after the cannibal conversation, giant birds . . . were they albatross? I'm an authority on birds of a different feather, you get me, mate? Ha-ha, a joke. Now, let me continue . . . These giant birds came to circle the ship with all the grace of native dancing girls. Beneath them skimmed a shoal of flying fish, and as I watched one by one the great birds fell from the sky to scoop them up. When they were finished, only a single fish floated belly-up in the now light, translucent, green water (it had changed overnight), in which the different colours of jellyfish, brown, purple, pink and rainbow hued pulsated like so many orchids. Carla came to my side and leant over the railing to point out a bluish specimen. She flashed a roguish grin at me, then dared me to dive over the side and bring it to her. I hummed and hawed. "I'm sure that the captain will heave to for a few minutes for you," she said, knowing that he would do anything for her. I replied that I might use a net, and she asked: "What is the name of that one . . . tell me?" I stared at the thing, what could I call it? Then, impelled by some bizarre need for honesty, I confessed: "I don't know!"

'The three words dropped from my mouth and tumbled into our wake where they floated like, well, like discovered lies. I stared at that damnable jellyfish and blurted out again, "No, I don't know, I really don't know," then my Aussie cunning came to my rescue and I added: "All I know is that it is an extremely poisonous species, and if those stings dangling below touched my bare skin it would be all over with me."

'My words startled her. She placed a hand on my shoulder and said: "Don't let it bother you. Relax, empty your mind for a moment and the name'll come to you. It always does."

'I nodded, though I missed whether she affirmed or denied that the species was poisonous. Later, I discovered it was and if I had taken up her dare and gone over the side, I might have ended belly-up like the flying fish. Still, the lack of a suitable name for the bloody thing upset me. I banged my fist on the railing and declared: "I don't know!"

'To this display of, of petulance, she smiled sympathetically and replied: "Even a scientist is not expected to know everything. You after all are a specialist?"

' "Still," I muttered sheepishly, hating to continue to lie to my fair companion, "it is close to my field and I should know."

'Then I heard my lying voice continue on in a sad parody of my life. I suffered from these blackouts. They threatened my career, no matter how hard I tried, the simplest things and concepts and precepts disappeared from my mind. "Why, sometimes," I said coming perilously close to the truth, "I almost fail to remember exactly what, or who I am."

' "But the Nobel Prize?" she hinted.

'And then I cursed myself, for the Japanese woman knew who I was and if she knew then this woman also did, or did she? She, she seemed so sympathetic. Bewildered by the contradiction, I continued to exaggerate towards the edge of inanity. For the life of me I couldn't tell this, this beauteous creature, the truth, I was stuck with my pelagic jelly, and so I, this skinny tall man in his checkered shorts and long white socks, muttered about the hardness of life when cursed by such an impediment. I even gave a wild laugh of despair, and all the recent events and humiliations which had been lurking in my subconscious drove me on.

' "So now you know that I'm not perfect, that I suffer from serious memory lapses, and you'll despise me," I cried, hating the sound of the whine entering into my voice. "Please, understand. It is hard, hard." And I buried my face in my hands and wondered if I could go on in this vein, for I felt no elation in leading this woman astray, or down the garden path. Perhaps you too find me despicable, and I confess that often I have found myself despicable. I can find no excuses for my past actions. I enjoyed cheating people, I enjoyed it and often found myself following a line of lies though my victim had ferreted out the truth from others. This was the case here too, but I was blinded by, by passion, so much so that I really believed myself to be a scientist and began pointing out the differences which distinguished that blue monstrosity from other jellyfish, though my only contact with such creatures was with the stingers that infested the Queensland coast in the summer season, and it was from them that I had formed the opinion that the blue in the jellyfish signified poison as it did in the stingers.

'Then my language fell away. Sentences became disjointed, verbs became lost, adjectives missed their nouns, clauses floated belly-up in the briny. I stuttered and sought for words like a toddler. I felt that I was crossing over that verge into the breakdown that I had so far avoided.

' "Terrible, terrible. A loss." Like a parrot mouthing empty phrases. "What am I saying? Please, let it be. Everything fine. Memory, you know, lapse. Jellyfish, pelgasmic jelly." Lie after lie. How to live like that? Sea. Ocean. Fish. Giant birds. Blue now green. Who flung that cat? A trap, trap. "Sorry, sorry for being, just being, like, well, you know, I expect you don't. Quite brilliant, really. My resumé. Why, I don't know? " . . . Did I ramble like that to her? I don't know. Then my language turned cloying: "You're so sweet, so understanding, so wholesome, so all that I am not, please be my salvation, my redemption! Don't turn your back on me, please don't."

'Carla stared at me while I carried on in this fashion. I shot glances at her to see how she was taking it. I thought I detected compassion in her eyes. Yes, I did, and the sympathy of that adorable woman made me exult in suffering. I saw astonishment combined with a joy that I had chosen her to reveal my weakness to. They love it, don't they, when a strong man collapses in emotional confusion? Now I saw a vast pity flowing with love for this poor academic. Yes, yes, it's true. At that moment, I swear I saw, I was absolutely sure that the woman loved me; but then, why do I also see, why do I remember something else, that her eyes flickered with malice and irony? Why, why, except that she knew my story was a complete pack of lies? But if this is so, why didn't she flee from me? Why did she stay and listen? Did she find some value in me? Were the bright red eyes of the *Kwinkan* winking out at her. Was she a *Gyinggi* woman anxious to trap me . . . who had trapped me? I'm sorry, I'm sorry, for this loss of control, it is, was then unusual. Ask any of my previous acquaintances and good time buddies, I was an able real estate broker, the best on the Gold Coast, then I lost all, and by all, I mean all.

'Finally I ran out of embellishments, and she said gently and simply: "I have read that genius is next to insanity, and in your case, it appears to be so . . . " Her voice trailed off into one whispered word. It was then she gave a little laugh as she took my hand and confided in me about a scientist who had come to the islands: "This scientist, one like you. The British

Government sent him out to our islands to overcome a sugarcane pest which was decimating our crop. He never ever settled down to work. Instead, he stayed on in our only town with my uncle and confined his researches to the rum we distilled. He eventually succumbed, succumbed to the rigours of our way of life. By then our sugarcane pest had long disappeared along with our crop. In a way this was a blessing, for it forced us to go into other, and more profitable, crops. In fact, because of our cultivation of rare and expensive oil plants, he was indirectly responsible for the founding of Sas Enterprises. You know, I have even named our research and development department after him."

'She gave that low little laugh again and her eyes filled with a voluptuousness as she took my face between her hands and stated: "You scumbag, you bullshit artist."

'I shuddered and tried to draw away my face, but her grip was strong. I stammered out: "Carla, Carla, please, I can't help it. I have been through trying times. My enemies have got me down. I am at the end of my tether." My fluttering hands touched her hips and clung. I felt her breasts quiver against my chest. I looked into her eyes which were almost level with mine as I brokenly quavered: "Carla, Carla, I love you, love me in return, please?"

'It was then I felt the *Kwinkan* stirring in my mind. It was he who answered the message of her body. I pressed myself against her and stayed there unable to move. She held me and I could not withdraw. It was then that I should have pulled away, should have raced to my cabin and locked myself in. I wasn't that far gone, I could have escaped; but no, I felt that she and I were of the same nature. I murmured how much I loved her and it was she who pushed me away. She looked me over and said: "I don't know. I'll talk to you later in your cabin."

'A flame of green fire leapt from her eyes and then she was gone leaving me badly shaken. I felt that I had lost something I needed. And what I needed then was a cold beer. I got it and returned to the deck. As I up-ended it into my mouth, I stared at the stubby masts which barely swayed, though they quivered owing to the vibration of the engine. I was like those masts, vibrating to the remembered touch of that glorious body. I became a man ready to engage in an affair. Somehow, the message had passed between us. I finished my tinny, then lent on the rail humming an absurd popular song about how love makes the world go 'round. I felt I had it all, but deep inside a laugh commenced and continued until I drowned it in another beer.

'I felt it was time I repaired to my cabin to await my dear visitor. I pushed open my door and stumbled into disarray. A businessman is always tidy. Someone had rifled my things. Shirts and socks and shoes and shorts were flung about. The bunk had been stripped and the mattress thrown onto the floor. What was I to make of it? I saw my empty upturned suitcase. I searched for my revolver. It was gone. I created more mess as I searched feverishly for it. Not only was it a means of protection, but I had had to sign for it, and one day the Government would exact its pound of flesh for its loss.

'It was then that a gentle knock touched my door. I opened it to reveal the smiling face of Carla. She pushed past me and exclaimed at the sight: "I knew that academics were messy, but this is positively diabolical. Why, I remember a professor in my university, he was dishevelled, but never like this." She was going to detail her experiences when a shot was fired. This was followed by two more in rapid succession. "Oh, my God!" I exclaimed and raced out onto the deck. I stopped in amazement, for there stood Miss Tamada with my .357 magnum in her small fist.

' "This gun is a cheap copy of the real thing," she stated. "It not only fires to the right, but high as well."

' "Does it?" replied Carla coming to her friend and taking the revolver from her hand. She adopted a firing stance, two hands clasped around the butt and knees bent. Miss Tamada tossed overboard one of my discarded tinnies. Carla sighted on it as it spun around in our wake. She let go three rapid shots at the target.

"You're right, Riyoko," she said. "I couldn't even hit that

can once. Obviously a cheap imitation, perhaps from Taiwan."
She passed the revolver to me and said: "Here, you try it."

'I raised my revolver and pressed the trigger. There was a click, it was all out of bullets and I had not brought any more with me. I turned to Miss Tamada and asked: "Where did you get this? It is mine."

' "Ah, that explains it," the Japanese woman replied. "Australian Government issue obviously."

'Was it that obvious? But I let the comment pass. Who could have searched my cabin and taken my gun? I did not believe that it was Miss Tamada. My suspicions settled on the captain. A rogue, if ever there was one.

' "Still, Miss Tamada," I said, "you haven't explained how you came into possession of this, this weapon. My cabin has been rifled and this was taken."

' "Oh it was lying on that table. I picked it up and when the cook tossed over the garbage, I decided to have a few shots. You know, you shouldn't leave loaded weapons lying around. Why, the safety catch wasn't even on."

'I raged with frustration. The beastly woman refused to answer my questions and continued to drag in extraneous material. Were, were all Japanese women so obtuse?

' "Oh come on," Carla said, "is it important? It isn't even a very good copy. You should consider yourself lucky that it did not explode in Riyoko's hands. If it did, think of the suit for damages. Poor dear," she murmured to Riyoki as she stroked her hands. "Dear, you shouldn't fire off strange weapons. At least, check to see if they are originals, rather than cheap copies."

' "But," Riyoko smiled, "I did check. It is made in one of our Taiwanese factories. We have quality control at least for the material, but I see that they should be test fired now. I'll pass on the information and the next time you find yourself firing a .357 Kitsune magnum, it shall fire true."

'I stared at my empty gun, then at the two women. If everything was possible as it seemed to be, they might even have some bullets. I was just about to ask them when a large hand reached out and took the revolver from me. "You ken, Laddy, these things are dangerous and I'll have none of them on my ship."

'He flung the revolver into the ocean and I stuttered and began to protest until he quoted a Fijian law, under which the schooner was registered, to the effect that unlicensed weapons were banned on ships. What could I do? I flung my hands up in despair and retreated to the saloon, where I, for want of a better term, hung one on. I remember in the course of the night going to my cabin and regarding the mess. My possessions were strewn across the floor like my discarded dreams. I could have cried, but instead went back to the saloon for a large whisky.

SESSION SIX

'Well, again we start. Ah, that stupid gun episode. How silly it seems now, or does it? Really an odd-shaped piece to fit into the puzzle. Yes; but to begin, to continue. The tape-recorder is consuming its tape and wants my words to spice its silence. It moves around and around, the voyage of that schooner endlessly circling in my mind, and the *Kwinkan*? Sir, put it down to a mere flight of fancy. Aboriginal substitutions, I mean, of course, superstitions do not sit well within the European mind; but I digress. Of course, my life is one long digression. Let it be; let it be . . . Well, after the pistol episode, it all seemed to fall away. You see, before then I felt I had it in the palm of my hand . . . Had what? Well, everything, sir, everything. Opportunities galore. Just recall, I was on a boat with an influential member of the Kitsune Corporation and the head of Sas Enterprises and she was not only that, but a member of the most influential family on a group of undeveloped islands soon to achieve, or be given, independence and thus presenting ripe pickings for one of my kind. Then Carla was also a good-looking screw, well worth a tumble on the mattress and, you know, get a woman in your bed, do your stuff and all else follows. Get me? Such opportunism, such opportunities, and just as I began reaching out, the cabin and gun business startled me and I jerked my hand back. It was then that things began to go wrong. Don't worry, I am about to get to them. Right now, in fact, for I dislike rambling on . . .

'Next morning, I could barely bring myself to face my fellow passengers. In fact, it was not a difficult thing to do, for Carla and Miss Tamada from then on were inseparable as well as most incommunicative. Abandoned to my own devices, I had no one to turn to, but the captain, who proved a gruff, old sea-dog with a surprising sense of humour. He loved my rendition of "A Scottish Soldier", and in the evenings we used to sit on deck, he sipping his whisky and I sucking on my beer while we eyed the two women discussing what they were discussing as they strolled around the deck arm in arm. Why, on occasion they even giggled like two schoolgirls. They brought a dab of colour into our dour men's world.

'I believe that if we had had more time, our little group might have re-formed in all its previous intimacy, but on the fifth morning I came on deck to find our sturdy vessel under the command of her doughty skipper chugging through a scattering of islands, all of a similar design as if they came from the factories of Kitsune: a circle of green marked with an indentation of white. A few were circled completely by reefs; while others shared a single *lei*. Of course being privy to the confidences of our skipper meant that I knew that on this day we would be among the islands. In fact, the previous night he had pointed the stem of his reeking pipe (naturally like all mariners he smoked a pipe rather than the too feminine cigarette) at the thick boll of a coconut palm drifting past and stated that we were close to our destination. Now we headed straight at a large green and red island which stood up from the water, if you will pardon the expression, like a rampant prick. It even had a head of sorts, being crowned by a pink and white cone of what, Carla had informed me of this when she and I were communicating, had once been an active volcano. It had been long dormant, but as I stared at it, I suddenly shivered as I imagined it spurting with, with the cum of red hot lava. In fact, so vivid was the image that I seemed to feel the splash of drops of warm fluid on my face. I gave a silly kind of laugh and looked around sheepishly, for I was standing at the bows and some drops of spray had been dashed up.

'Moving right to the very tip of the bow, I assumed a position much like the figurehead ornamenting the bows of a vessel, though I had always thought these to be female. Leaning forward, I stared directly at real life and the beginning of my mission. On that somewhat grotesque island stood a general post office and a mailbox. There was communication with Australia and details about how to further my mission. Now shipboard life became unreal and my lies to Carla ceased to matter. Shipboard life was as ephemeral as shipboard romance. Now I wanted to see a newspaper and check the Brisbane stockmarket. I wanted to be in contact with the wider world and my broker. I forgot that this vessel was the mail boat and the only newspapers I might see would be a week old, the ones I had already glanced through in Suva. Still, still for all I knew, amongst the mail might be my instructions. I would be directed to contact a shadowy so-and-so, have secret meetings in the night with the Opposition, be privy to the mysterious comings and goings of shrouded beings plotting for the seizure of power and above all booty. It was then that I knew that I was the man for the job. I could plot with the best of them when it came to the dollar. Then doubts arose. The image of Carla with the flashing green eyes and delectable mouth rose to taunt me. Could I really betray her and curry favour with the Opposition? Of course I damn well could. I really believed it—then!

'I had never been captured by a woman. My creed was to take 'em then leave 'em when I got what I came for. It was a good philosophy and I should have stuck to it. Of course, I have been married twice, and almost thrice; but these alliances were dissolved when my needs were satisfied. A woman after all was a bad substitute for a mate on whom you could rely. And so I tried to see Carla in this light, though, I must admit, I had not attained my objective; but when the opportunity came again, I would take her for all I could get. It never entered my mind, and in fact I could not believe, that I might become an infatuated slave ready to obey the slightest whim of my mistress, and worse, to be manipulated by such a harridan. How could I believe this, especially when I populated the approaching island with willing golden girls hot with the urgency of the tropics? It was then that my fickle imagination betrayed me. I imagined Carla and her swooning rapture. I could feel her devouring lips on mine and the pressure of her thighs about me. Such an exquisitely shaped body writhing in pleasure and experiencing it in such powerful spasms that I had an erection. I heard her tiny cries, her long sigh suddenly choked off, a snatch of song falling from her lips in the afterglow. I tried to wrench my mind free from such images. The *Gyinggi* woman repelled as well as fascinated me. Such revulsion; such ecstasy. I felt the *Kwinkan* coming in great spasms which tore his flesh and drained the very marrow from his bones. Oh God, such fantasies, such such absurd fantasies. I stared out at the reefs bringing myself to some reality. The vessel passed close to one of them. The foam swirled exposing the hidden rocks beneath. The engines shuddered towards a passageway and my mouth twisted in mockery at myself and my emotions. What did it matter, they would crash into the reality of the approaching island, green and red with a pale cone of ice reaching up to cool the heaven of hot illusion. I struggled to free myself of carnal desires, for there in front of me lay the means to recoup my fortune.

'The ocean pulsed gently, calmly, radiantly behind me. A soft breeze flowed from our destination. It bore the aroma of slightly rotten bananas and the burnt musk of sugar. It was then that Carla joined me. I was alone with her, but too late . . . She smiled and touched my side. My eyes met hers. Under the golden red of her flowing hair, I saw a frown lying there in wrinkled lines of ivory across her forehead. I saw that her eyes were sad; then she tossed her head in that familiar gesture I had admired, and whispered: "Already, and, and I expected more from you."

' "It is never too late," I replied brightly.

' "Perhaps it is always too late, for you," she said flatly, her hand going to her dishevelled hair which was being tugged about by the breeze. One hand managed to encircle the glossy mass, the other fumbled at a silver clip. She raised her hands to fasten her hair and her upraised arms made her breasts swell. I could not drag my eyes away. Her hands left her head, her arms fell, and I saw that she had imprisoned her hair, pinned it back so severely that her face looked stern and bare. It was then that I could imagine her dominating her directors in the boardroom.

'But appearances were deceiving. Her eyes, flecked with gold, held mine as she spoke in a tiny voice so unlike her usual tone that I thought Miss Tamada had stolen up on us. She whispered: "What do you think about it?"

'I entered her mood, whatever it was and replied: "I don't know."

'She bit savagely down on her swollen bottom lip as she said: "We have to . . . " What on earth was she alluding to? It was beyond me. I waited for more words.

' "Do you know that the *Tui-tui* reaches port this afternoon? It'll stay for a few days, then return to Suva. Did you know that?"

' "Yes," I replied, for the skipper had told me so.

' "Well, then, perhaps you should be on it. Our islands really are still pretty dull, and perhaps your, your mission might be somewhat upsetting for us."

' "Never, Carla, never," I couldn't help exclaiming.

' "Still, we are somewhat insular and don't take kindly to strangers snooping around. We like to pick our own friends . . . "

' "Carla, you can trust me. I would never do anything to hurt you, never, never."

' "And yet," she said with a malicious smile, "you have ignored me for the last few days. You seemed to find that captain more to your taste. Well, I didn't think you were like that!"

' "Like what?" I almost shouted.

' "Well, no matter," she said shrugging my question away. "Your mission, well, perhaps it is not that important."

'I felt myself wilting under her gaze. Desperately, I began to stress the importance of my mission, declaring that it would bring our two countries together and that I had the confidence of the Prime Minister.

' "I see," she replied dispassionately. "I welcome you to our island as a respected guest. Soon, you will be able to see the small island on which Kitsune is building our international airport. It is of utmost importance for us to have it. Our future, I feel, is in tourism and for that we need an airport and one close to the capital, though somewhat isolated from it. Do you think terrorism will ever come to our lovely island?" she asked, suddenly clutching my arm. "Sometimes, sometimes, I'm so afraid of the future, so afraid."

'I took the opportunity to clasp her to me, as she continued: "You see, darling, please forget your Brisbane, Sydney and Canberra. Things are different on our islands. My family have been colonial rulers for 200 years. Little Britain so far away, left us to our own devices. Do you realise," she said with a grin, detaching herself from my arms, "that we never have had a royal visit, not a single one? We have always been passed by. In fact, I feel that the Colonial Office in London must have misplaced our file until recently and so we are used to making our own laws, not only for ourselves but for the other people here. We are used to ruling and used to that freedom which comes from ruling. You and others limit yourselves to petty intrigues and hypocrisies; but we have never had the need, or the need to lie as you have lied to me. You are so used to lying that you lie to yourself constantly. You lie to yourself and to others in order to rob them, then lie again to cover up your crime. I can feel nothing but contempt for such a system and those trapped within it," she said with a grimace which made her face ugly.

' "But, but . . . " I exclaimed.

' "Don't 'but' me, I pass through such edifices of lies and return to the honesty of my own home. This is mine, all mine; but how unfortunate that we too must think about stooping to subterfuge in order to maintain my, our independence."

' "Oh Carla, oh Carla," I whispered, forgetting the businesswoman to reach out for the soft, island girl beneath, "let me cherish and protect you. You're such a sweet kid, so so unspoilt."

' "Oh God," she exclaimed impatiently, "you are such a boy. I would have thought that with all your manipulations in the world of finance, you might offer me something concrete; but you are like all your countrymen where women are concerned: naive!"

'Well, naturally, I recoiled. She might be the head of Sas Enterprises, a glorified string of beauty salons and thus suitable for a woman; but I was a man from the male world of business and not only that but an Aussie. And this woman hailing from an obscure group of islands which placed altogether would be less than the size of Tasmania, had called me naive.

'She saw the look on my face, but refused to see reason. "Just remember," she said, "that everything is simple here. These islands are ours and always will be. I invite you here, and through me you shall have an entrance into our society, but don't assume too much . . . " She smiled into my scowl and exclaimed: "I expect that you'll be making reports. Well, I will wish to see them before you send them off. This has nothing to do with you, darling," she added, relenting a little, "but it will be for the best. Will you promise me at least that?" she asked imploringly.

'Who can resist the importuning of a beautiful woman? I promised.

' "Thank you, thank you darling," she murmured in return, her eyes soft and misty. "You know, I have a place on the side of the mountain. I designed it to, well to cater for my every whim. I had it spun from concrete, so light so ethereal; but when I tire of being there, of being perfect as it were, I leave to seek other diversions. Now, I can't wait to get back to my nest. You shall come there with me. We'll construct your reports there. You'll be the perfect little spy, no, you disagree with the term, well, agent. Now, don't shake your head and look stern. You have little to complain about. You'll be seen to be doing your job and no one'll be the wiser. Say 'yes', please say 'yes'," she demanded like a small child.

' "But, but, Carla," I began.

' "But what?" she demanded, stamping her foot in exasperation. "There are no 'buts' on my island. You're going there and that's that."

' "Yes, maybe . . . perhaps for a few days."

' "Well, that wasn't hard, was it," she said sardonically. "God, you Aussies are so British sometimes that you remind me of the New Zealanders. So it's settled. My uncle, you'll like him, he's a scientist like you pretended to be, is Resident, we never rated a Governor, at Hermansburg, our soon-to-be capital. You can stay in his official residence before we move up onto the mountain."

'I nodded just as Miss Tamada came up lugging her damnable computer. She got Carla to sit on the deck cross-legged by her side and soon the machine was humming and flickering with plans and images of the new airport. The Japanese woman ignored me and kept her voice down as she pointed out parts of diagrams to Carla, then if a detail seemed obscure, she isolated it and increased its size to fill the screen. Such were the marvels of modern Japanese technology, but I soon grew bored. My mind was on other things.

'I stared at some outrigger canoes which drifted past us, or rather went on with their fishing while we nosed past them. A few sails showed in the gap in the reef towards which we were heading. Beyond I saw the white roofs of Hermansburg. Somehow, I recognised it as colonial. In fact it reminded me of a mid-nineteenth-century etching I had seen of the penal settlement of Van Diemen's Land. It looked just as small and just as desolate. As I stared a sense of foreboding came over me, just as it must have come over those poor convicts who came up on the decks of their prison ships to see their future homes and realised that they were as far away from civilisation as they could be sent. This is what the Prime Minister had done to me.

'The vessel nosed through the gap in the reef and entered what was quite a large harbour. Beneath me Miss Tamada tapped out a code which resulted in pictures of what Hermansburg would eventually become. Kitsune had big plans for this island, huge plans, and all I had was sweet f.a. The schooner began manoeuvring towards the wharf. A group of islanders clustered looking up at me. Their eyes got to me and

I glanced away towards a smaller island enclosed within the reef. It had been rendered down into a flat platform of coral on which moved a solitary yellow bulldozer. The new airport. I shrugged and went to my cabin to pack.'

SESSION SEVEN

'Now, where was I in this, this continuing story of betrayal? Just about to disembark from the schooner? Yes, that's it. I went to my cabin and finished packing my suitcase, then checked around to make sure that I had not left anything behind. Only an old *Bulletin*, but I had no use for that. I hefted my case and made for the gangplank. Since the incident of my cabin being searched and my revolver misappropriated, I had decided to keep my possessions in my hands. I didn't want any of those thieving Lascars running off with my things . . . Lascar, you don't know the term? What, mate, you haven't read Sax Roehmer and his books on the devious Fu Manchu? You missed more than a good read. He was the one who introduced me to the devious Lascar. Who, or what is he? Well, how would I know? I didn't live in Victorian times, some sort of villainous oriental, I expect. What, an East Indian seaman? Well does it matter, after all they do look all alike, don't you think? You don't? Well I do, mate, and I've had the experience. Anyway, enough of Lascars, they have very little to do, to do with my narrative, that's what this is, a narrative, isn't it? No, I don't want to get into any discussion on what constitutes a narrative. Who cares about such theories, except persons such as yourself?

'I hefted my suitcase to the gangplank, put one foot on it, then the other, and suddenly I found myself falling. The bloody thing had given away. Down, I went, and before I knew it I was in the water between the side of the boat and the wharf, another solid wall. All it took was a bit of a swing and I would've been crushed in between them. In fact, I saw the vessel coming in towards me. The gap narrowed. This was it, I thought, then there were shouts and the schooner was pushed away. A rope was flung down to me and a very wet and angry me was dragged out to confront the calm face of the skipper, who took the stem of his pipe from out his mouth (God, the nerve of him) and said: "Dash it, laddy, you should take more care."

' "How could I when the bloody thing collapsed under my feet?" I shouted.

'I was about to give him a piece of my mind when a giggle made me look to where Carla and that infernal Miss Tamada stood trying to keep the grins off their faces. It wasn't funny. No it wasn't, and the carelessness of one of those Lascars, for who else could it have been, had almost caused my death.

' "Oh you do get into the most dreadful scrapes," Carla exclaimed, trying to control her mirth.

' "He is a very wet one, that one," exclaimed Miss Tamada.

'I stood there dripping in front of them. At least, the weight of my suitcase told me that water had not filled it.

' "You better come along with us to the Residency," Carla told me. "You can have a shower there, and if you haven't got dry clothing, I'm sure that Uncle will lend you some . . . Boy, it sure was funny. There one moment, oops gone the next," and she broke into peals of laughter which spread among the onlookers. I was the centre of wild guffaws. It didn't help things to learn that the natives had a sense of humour, especially when it was directed at me.

'We shoved off in a little convoy of mirth. We were followed by a crowd who pointed me out to those who had not been there. I tried to put the best face on things. It could have been worse, for the heat was torrid, and my little dip had been a godsend. The town wasn't anything to write home about either. A collection of tin shacks and a few construction sites about a bank, a post office and a large store—soon to be a shopping centre—all owned by Carla, or her family. In my uneasy state, I smiled cynically as I thought about the future independent nation. From what I could see of the inhabitants, they seemed to have nothing to do, except to marvel at us as we passed along like scraps of European culture and artifacts which had come ashore. We drifted past what Carla told me was the pride of the town, a large cinema hall which also contained a radio station which she informed me gave out only local news. She said that apart from that it broadcast only the most insipid of island music interspersed with hymns of the Christian sect which, she again told me, a great-grandfather of hers had introduced into the islands. The inhabitants quickly accepted it as their own and produced their own ministers to ensure the purity of transmission. I shrugged; but still she went on, and with a straight face.

'She said that the great-grandfather had acquired the status of a saint and that in the main church and the chapels scattered over the islands, prayers of thanksgiving were offered to him who had first brought the light to them. What had their religious beliefs to do with me? Let them believe what they like as long as it did not concern me. To get away from such absurdities, I asked her about her uncle, the Resident of this isolated colony of an empire decayed to a few such dreary places. It appeared that London had long since ceased to care about the island chain and was content to the point of inertia to accept an official who did not demand a salary, or pass on demands for development funds. The British were relieved, that is if they had occasion to notice, or even to recall (remember the lost file?), that, and this is what Carla assured me, no vocal independence movement had arisen to demand compensation and aid. I shrugged and accepted her words, for when I thought about this island chain, which wasn't very often in these first few days, the notion that Australia (or Japan for that matter, what on earth was the Kitsune Corporation doing there?) was interested in the place appeared ludicrous. In fact, just being there made me fall into moods of despondency (one occasioned by discovering a huge scorpion in my bed, though the island was supposed not to harbour such monsters) during which I cursed the Prime Minister for sending me there to rot. What made it worse was that the town was unbearably hot, and it didn't help my mood to be told by the uncle, who once upon a time had been a true-blue Brit, that the island quickly killed off any Europeans foolhardy enough to make it their home.

I did not ask though, that if that was the case, why it had
not happened to the old creep himself. He would have smiled
and waffled on about genes and things. He was that sort of
bore.

'He had the gift of the gab and all that I had to do was
listen. I learnt too much about my posting, the field of my
endeavours as it were, Christ! There were a number of
plantations run by obsequious Fijian Indians, or dubious
persons of mixed blood. The uncle, who had the only air-
conditioned coolness in town, also had a well-oiled system of
information in which the original inhabitants were the links.
The Indians were, the word had long since degenerated into
a signifier of terror, pagans, and in fact they were deliberately
kept so and a temple had been constructed in which they could
worship their strange multi-armed gods. This led the inhabitants into some absurd beliefs, even to the extent that they
saw themselves as good Christians groaning in slavery under
a harsh pagan tyranny supported and kept in place by Rome.
How Rome and India came to be identified together, is for
the ethnologist to fathom. And another of their beliefs, which
kept things quiet so that I suspected it as a piece of propaganda
invented by Carla's family past or present, was that they would
suffer this for a thousand years before a Christ hero would
arrive with fire and brimstone from the suddenly awakened
volcano to elevate his followers and to send the heathens to
the bottom of the social pile where they would remain as slaves
for all eternity. The uncle told me all this with many a chuckle.
"We'll be long gone before then," he would repeat, for he was
in the habit of repeating and repeating and repeating things,
and then he would repeat his chuckles until they threatened
to choke him. Oh God, what a hole I had fallen into.

'Well, you can see that I had settled in at the Residency and
that after my first undignified appearance, things had gone well
enough for me, except Carla was hardly to be seen. Miss
Tamada dragged her here and there about the town along with
that awful computer. Big plans were afoot, but the heat outside
was too much to bear and I preferred to rest in the coolness,

though this meant I had to endure the repetitions. Once, after another long-winded conversation, spiced with chuckles, about the religious beliefs of the natives (who if they had had any sense would have forgotten about the poor Indians and tossed this old fool into the drink and then made sure that he never came up) I said to him: "But what part does Carla play in this rigmarole?"

' "Carla, Carla, Carla," he iterated. "Natural, natural, only natural that you ask. Ask and you shall receive, eh what? But in this case, asking is not receiving, for to be precise, though with hesitations, and with a greater or lesser degree of honesty, I must answer you to the extent that I am able, which is to be unable. I, for one, do not know. The islanders, the natives, the people here, the indigenes who have told me that they derive, or have their origins from the last eruption of that volcano, the date undetermined, but alluded to in Genesis in Carla's great-grandfather's, on the maternal side, translation and as eternally quoted by their ministers, or parsons, or preceptors as: 'The rock laboured, fire issued and brought forth men.' Well, now, I feel I should answer your question, what was it?"

'I repeated the question and then drank down the rest of my gin and lime, for there was no beer on the island and I had had to resort to spirits. Oh, damn, even now, long after the event, his enunciation still enters my head. It was often unendurable, but I endured it until I found myself formulating the same sentences.

' "Ah, yes, yes, the ministers and their, their flock, or should it be flocks, perhaps congregations, but it does not fit, well, although they are already to inform us, to tell us, to detail at great and often wearisome length, the alleged doings, though more often misdoings of the pagans, the heathen to be precise; well, they, the ministers and their flock, should it be singular or plural, seldom, yes, rarely refer to us, and by us, I mean myself, Carla and other members of our family, even to the extent that they pretend to, or be in ignorance of, or prevaricate about the place our enlightened ancestor holds in their theology, and how this affects his progeny and affiliates like myself. Perhaps, to be imprecise, or to, using a colloquialism, hazard a guess, we are of the elect, seeing, or as it happens we are descended, myself indirectly and Carla directly from He who was responsible for bringing them the Gift of Light. Ah, sir, such a noble gift, a rare gift, you can't buy that at Harrods, not even in those days, and as for these days, well Carla tells me, worse days, worse days . . . Perhaps, to end it, to finish it, to gloss over it, we are seen as part of that Godhead and thus beyond their comprehension—perhaps, for I don't know."

'I muttered under my breath "codswallop", for no one, and surely not any of the locals could believe such, such drivel. On a foray out into the wilderness of the streets, I had been accosted by one of these so-called natives who had sold me of all things an Australian Aboriginal boomerang. He claimed that his people had invented it, and on returning to my air-conditioned shelter I turned it over to find a cryptic stamp which revealed that it had been made by Boonah Enterprises, Cairns, Queensland. I doubt that such a villain could have accepted this old dodderer as part of some such absurdity labelled "Godhead".

'But, but what was this baloney to me? I strove to push away my uncharitable thoughts as he pressed on me the excellent gin and lime which he again assured me was the drink for the tropics. After a few, I could not but agree with him and we were happily ensconced in the coolness mumbling obscurities and repetitions at each other as we downed the drinks . . .

'Solid land beneath my feet, the relief from the heat and my pleasant time indoors, not forgetting the numberless gin and limes which eventually made me see the Resident through a blue alcoholic daze, made me recover my good spirits, though I did not feel the urge for action of any kind. Still, when I was not with the Resident, with gin and lime in hand, I reclined in a cane lounger and went over my old coups and thus began to rebuild my confidence. Hermansburg from the shelter of the Residency appeared a city of opportunities. Going over and over this in my mind, how repetition grows on one, I decided

to stroll the length of the main street and being the tourist
stared at the people, some of whom in skin colouring and
bodily structure reminded me of gingerbread men. Later on,
I was to learn the reason for their appearance, but not then.
I met and bought my island artifact, the boomerang, from an
affable merchant, who told me he was refining his skills for
the soon-to-be coming hordes of tourists and thanked me for
allowing him to practise on me. He even insisted that I sign
his visitors book. I scrawled an obscenity and escaped his dismal
shop, to duck down two or three drab little lanes ostensibly
in order to make for a beach, but really in search of those golden
voluptuous women skilled in the practices of love which that
painter fellow, Gangrene or some such name, had painted, and
which I saw in an exhibition in the Queensland Cultural Centre
when I was trying to do a deal with a most boring bloke who
insisted on pointing out the features of the pictures as art when
all I was interested in were the women depicted in them.

'So much for fancy and so much for art. The few women
I came across were like women the world over. We had better
and prettier specimens in Surfers'. I was so put out by the lack
of the nubile females I had imagined that on one remembered
evening when Carla and Miss Tamada joined us for dinner,
I tried a few coarse jests on the matter.

'Miss Tamada wrinkled her nose in that disgusting habit
of hers and Carla raised her eyebrows. Such was the reception
of my *bon-mots* that I quickly dropped the subject, having no
wish to wound either of the women's feelings, or to be thought
vulgar, so instead I began a discreet lampooning of the
Resident.

'Carla looked at me thoughtfully, then inquired: "Why are
you so cheerful? You used to be so, so—how shall I put it
without hurting your feelings—morbid, but now you are the
very life of the party. Perhaps you should make gin and lime
your drink, for certainly it has a better effect on you than beer."

' "Perhaps, he should try poison," muttered Miss Tamada,
"for his wit certainly needs putting to death."

' "You little old grouch," I gently mocked her. "You know

what they say about oriental women?"

'Yes, that we make excellent businesswomen and make the most of opportunities unlike some men . . . "

' "Riyoko, Riyoko," laughed Carla, "and you know what they say about girls who work all the time and never play?"

' "No, what do they say?"

' "They become bad lays."

' "Oh, do you think that?" and the two women exchanged secretive smiles that I found disconcerting.

'Now something occurred which I had been dreading. Carla had urged me to carry on my pretence of being a scientist. I demurred and she asked me again. I refused, then she said that her uncle would grow suspicious if I could not convince him that I had a legitimate purpose for being on the island. "He after all is the sole person for determining who is or is not allowed to stay, and as he is somewhat cantankerous and inclined towards suspicion of Australians, he might very well order you to leave on the *Tui-tui*." I agreed with some trepidation, for the uncle, at least according to Carla, had been a scientist of some renown before he came to the island, and this made me wonder how I could successfully carry off my imposture when he most likely had all the facts at his fingertips so to say. I breathed a little easier when she assured me that Sir Joseph had forgotten everything as he had pickled his brain in gin.

'Now the time had come. "I believe, I declare, or rather I have heard that you are an embryologist," he said. I waited believing I was in for it. A mild relief came as Carla turned to Miss Tamada and whispered: "They certainly are a strange pair."

' "What?" I said.

' "An embryologist?" he repeated in wonder.

' "What do you get when you put one pair with another pair?" Miss Tamada whispered to Carla.

' "Odd balls," Carla suggested.

' "*Pairpair*, which means in . . . '

'But I was looking at Sir Joseph as I nodded. He certainly

was a weird one. He was short and stout, so different from my long and lean look. His face was sallow and dried out with a few strands of hair dangling from his chin. It was a face which made others swear off growing beards, and I never shaved as closely as I did when I was staying there. Sir Joseph also had long gone troppo and eschewed the proper tropic dress as worn in Queensland of open-neck shirt, shorts and long socks and shoes, or if not this a safari suit. These were the acceptable canons of dress and I kept to them. But this man who was an official of the British Government and supposedly ruled the island, wore a sarong draped loosely over his paunch and a once-white singlet over his sunken chest. He really was a sight to be endured only with liberal effusions of gin and lime. In looking at him, it was difficult to avoid conclusions being drawn about the beauty or lack of it in the human race.

'Well, I was sitting with the two giggling women in a low cane chair conscious of how his knees pushed like cucumbers, giant zucchinis, marrows, or something like that against the sarong cloth, when he had potted the question, to which I had nodded.

' "He repeated: "An embryologist, eh?" Then he swished the ice cubes around in the bottom of his glass and called to the boy who looked after him to come and replenish his drink . . . and mine. While this was being done, he declared with some satisfaction: "An embryologist, eh?"

'Not only the "eh", question or statement, but the tone of satisfaction struck me. He had been waiting for such an expert to show up, had he some sort of project requiring such a scientist? Thus I asked myself, though I should have asked: what was the reason for the satisfaction? But that is not my way, I always jump to conclusions, and this time I jumped the wrong way.

'He made a gesture as if catching flies, then repeated and added and elaborated: "Embryologist? You are, eh? Like this, in the wood, up on the mountain, catching little butterflies, tra-la, tra-la. Bright gaudy butterflies spread out and stuck with pins. That little girl claims, she is a fox," and he pointed at Miss Tamada.

'She snarled and wriggled her nose and darted what was certainly a feral look at me; but what had this to do with embryology? "Yes," I said as if in agreement, then switched: "But it is more in the classification, don't you think?"

'I expected him as a scientist to agree, for once in a company of scientists holidaying on the Gold Coast, I had been almost bored to tears with their conversation, but I had learnt that scientists always looked on classification as the science and considered that pure research, or the collecting of specimens, was nothing else but an excuse for a research grant to buy the most expensive computers and the most complex software in order to create the most elegant form of what essentially was a list.

'The bait was not taken. He replied: "Very interesting, of the utmost interest is the Japanese belief in werefoxes. Werefoxes, such a, well, such a treat for an old man. Little teeth nibbling. Pretty things, foxes."

' "A fox has a tight box," said Miss Tamada in a serious voice.

' "Yes, but the teeth, the little nibbling teeth. Curious, very curious. An old man's joy." And his chin waggled up and down and his mouth moved, but no words came.

'The boy returned to refresh our glasses. Sir Joseph absently took a huge swallow, then pulled himself up from his cane chair. The chairs were like traps and once in them, it was difficult to get out. He had confided in me that this type of seating was best for the tropics as they provided an armrest to support his drinking arm on and a womb-like feeling that made for security. He reached down, grabbed my hand in his and pulled me to my feet without strain, then he took me into his office and to a heavy Chinese cupboard on the top of which stood three busts each crowned with a plastic lily. He pointed at the first: "Charles Darwin, a great naturalist, a very great naturalist, yes?"

' "Of course," I quickly agreed. It had been a question on a quiz show, the compere of which I had met at Jupiter's where

75

I watched him lose more than a few thousand dollars at roulette.

'The strange bird nodded wisely, then pointed to the second bust: "Mr Haeckel, another great naturalist, not as great as Darwin, but still great. This one liked little nibbling fish, little fish like butterflies," he added with a smirk.

' "Yes, yes a great man," I stated, then added, "though not as great as the master." To tell the truth, I had never heard the name before and still do not know who or what he was. Perhaps one day I might look it up in a biographical dictionary, but why? Haeckel, more likely Heckel and Jeckel, for the old bloke was ready for the loony bin.

'Sir Joseph placed his dried-out paw next to the lily on top of the remaining bust and declared with a shout: "Sir Richard Burton, the greatest naturalist of them all. His *Perfumed Garden* is superb, but he never reached Japan where the girls bloom like lotuses and the werefoxes gambol under the full moon. But still superb and far above such base imitators as Mirabeau and his *Pleasure Garden*."

'I hastened to agree, for Richard Burton was indeed a fine actor with a fine taste in women. Why, the eyes of Elizabeth Taylor were almost as beautiful as those of Carla.

'He took me back to the women who were chitchatting about womanly things. I excused myself and went to my room. When I arrived I checked for my mouth refreshers and then for some unaccountable reason, I pulled down the sheet on my bed. Someone was playing a practical joke on me, for there lurked the strangest prawn I had ever seen. Well, the island did breed weird and wonderful characters like Sir Joseph, so why not strange prawns? I decided to play a trick on Carla, perhaps push it down the back of her dress. I would enjoy watching her squirm. I was about to pick it up when it moved. There seemed to be some sort of sting on its tail, so I manoeuvred it into a water tumbler and carried it back to the others. Miss Tamada stared at me as I entered. Carla looked up and saw the glass. "What have you there?" she asked.

"Only a live prawn," I grinned and went to upturn the glass into my hand.

"Don't, don't, it's a deadly scorpion," Sir Joseph exclaimed, quickly taking the glass from me and covering it with a plate.

' "Are you sure?" Carla asked, peering at the glass. "We don't have scorpions on the island."

' "My dear, it's certain. My doctoral dissertation was on scorpions and this is one of the most deadly."

'I turned pale and began shaking. Carla came to me and put an arm around me: "Oh darling, you could have got a nasty bite," she said. I shuddered and agreed. Someone was out to get me, and alone and without aid, they most likely would. I had to get to a place of safety; but where?'

SESSION EIGHT

'I'm sorry that I had to terminate the last session. Even now thinking of that frightful insect gives me the willies. It is not often that one comes face to face with death; and not often that you realise that you have become a target of enemies unknown . . . And you say that Haeckel was a nineteenth-century German biologist, a follower of evolution and a supporter of Darwin's theory? Well, it means nothing to me, absolutely nothing. And that Sir Richard Burton was not the actor, but the famous explorer and eroticist? But the bust was the spitting image of the film star and after all, well wasn't he also an eroticist and an explorer of beautiful women? Sorry, I jest, I jest. Great actor, Burton; great woman, Elizabeth, at least in her prime. And this Mirabeau? A French writer, and naturally of dirty books. Well, enough of these, these old timers. What were they to me when I had discovered a poisonous insect in my bed?

'I was filled with apprehension. Wouldn't you have been? Worse, I began adding up the incidents: the flung moggy, my cabin being searched and my revolver being appropriated; the gangplank giving way under me, and now the poisonous insect. Someone was, or some people were, out to get me; but who, who? I could dismiss the old dodderer and dear sweet Carla, but Miss Riyoko Tamada was definitely a suspect. Still, who could believe that a prominent Japanese businesswoman would stoop to attempted murder? It didn't seem possible; but stranger things have happened, and that story she had told . . . Yes, definitely a suspect! Then the *Tui-tui* was still in port, supposedly hanging about owing to engine repairs. The old sea-dog, a suspect? Difficult to believe; but not impossible. A member of his crew, one of those Lascars, more than possible. I racked my brains throughout the night and reached the conclusion that perhaps members of some freedom movement on the island had mistakenly judged me to be a supporter of the ruling family. Could they be engineering the murder of an Australian diplomat, albeit one without the appropriate credentials, to score media attention? Yes, they could! I needed my revolver for protection. I cursed the captain for depriving me of it. Why, he might be part of the very gang plotting my death . . .

'A sleepless night did not help my mood and before breakfast I had a quick gin and lime to settle my nerves. It helped and I was more than relieved to be told by Carla that we were to go to her house on the mountain that very day. I would have liked to be rid of Miss Tamada, but alas she was accompanying us and I would have to remain on guard. At least the house was above such things as heat and mosquitoes. In my relief, I recalled that I had another reason to look forward to going there. Once, when I had complained about the lack of comeliness in the island women, Carla had spoken about a beautiful woman who took care of her bungalow when she was absent. She had featured as a model in a number of Sas ads, and as they only employed the most ravishing of females, I was all agog to see this creature. I expected her to meet us when our car pulled up in front of the modern bungalow half-dug into the mountain slope, but there was no sign of her. Servants, both islander and Indian there were; but no beautiful Maria. After we had settled in without undue incident, I casually mentioned her. Carla turned solemn and informed me that she had died.

' "Died?" I jerked out. "But she was young, in her late teens, or early twenties. Come on," I said, trying for levity, "you're having me on. Where is she?"

' "I truly wish I could produce her, but she is really and truly dead. She left me while I was away." She said this with such solemnity and with tears starting into her beautiful eyes that I could not but believe her. Miss Tamada, who was in the room with us, went to her and held her for a long while. I looked on embarrassed, for the scene was one of some intimacy; but then women are always hugging and fondling one another. They are soft physical creatures, unlike us men, aren't they?

'The interior of Carla's bungalow reflected her femininity, being furnished with a degree of soft luxury which I had not seen before. The furnishings there positively reeked of the decadent, as did, for that matter, the clothing which the two women changed into as soon as they arrived. Miss Tamada had dressed in a flowing kimono which could only remind me of the waitresses in the Japanese restaurants along the Gold Coast and Carla had on some sort of sheer, shimmering silk thing which draped her figure admirably. She had tried to get me into a sarong; but I resisted and settled for shorts and T-shirt and casual thongs. I seemed the odd person out as I gazed at the two women clinging to each other on a wide, silk-covered divan which Carla had informed me (she was a great one for information) had been the love couch of the Maharajah of Jaipur or some such place in India. I had to sit on a low cushion as there were no chairs and thus was on the level of Carla's nasty little Pekinese which had welcomed me into the house by taking a piece out of my ankle. Now it reposed beside the divan with its swollen eyes staring at me. It marked my every move with a little move of its own which kept me on my guard.

'Well, with the description out of the way, I should, I must return to the sad bereavement.

'Carla finally pulled herself together and raised a tear-stained face in which her green eyes shone like pieces of the finest jade. "I'm sorry, so sorry about it all, darling. I felt awful, really awful when I was told. You must have noticed how out of sorts I was in Hermansburg, just as you must have noticed some of those poor creatures with their limbs all puffed up. Such a sadness, such an affliction. Miss Tamada has sent a report back on the *Tui-tui* and she is certain that the Kitsune Corporation will dispatch a medical team to end the malady once and for all. Such a tragedy . . . "

"You mean the gingerbread men?" I exclaimed.

' "Well, that is a bit facetious. They suffer from a variant of elephantiasis. It does awful things to human bodies, especially to male bodies . . . "

' "My God, you don't mean that I might catch it?" Visions of my limbs swollen to the proportions of a Russ Hinze flashed into my mind, and there was no escape for by now the *Tuitui* would have sailed. "Why wasn't I told of this?" I demanded.

' "No need to feel concerned about your own pretty body, darling," she said tartly. "It is endemic to the islands, but cases have only been found among the native population and some of the Indians. There is not one single case of a European or a mixed blood having come down with it. If you want to see it as anything, see it as a racial pox . . . "

' "Thank God, thank God," I exclaimed, though still keeping my options open. If there was one disease there might be other virulent ones ready to attack those without immunity.

' "Somehow," and Carla began snivelling again, "Maria caught the disease and she found it terrifying. You know, everything can be terrifying in the tropics: love and hatred, illness and even health, bloom and decay, stress and relaxation. You know I loved her so, so very much. She was so beautiful in that superlative fashion which I strive for in Sas advertising and which I rarely find. I found it in her. I wept and wept when I heard what had happened . . . "

'She broke down again, and Miss Tamada took her into her arms. I watched uneasily. Finally, she quieted and Miss Tamada ceased her physical comfortings, staring at me as if I were an intruder before talking to her in a soft voice. "You know," she said, speaking to me as much as to Carla, "sometimes it is better that a friendship ends abruptly and finally. I am not being cruel, far from it. I remember that my relationship with my friend, Kumi, became weaker and weaker, and as it became weaker and weaker it also became virulent and inclined towards hatred. We avoided each other. Eventually, I couldn't stand the separation and one Sunday I went to her door. It was locked. I knocked, but it continued to stand between us as a barrier. I saw that the door was locked from the inside and so she must be inside, so I kept on knocking and knocking. I called out 'Kumi!' No reply. I shouted, 'Kumi, Kumi!' Suddenly, the door opened. She stood there in only her underwear. Nana was hanging onto her waist. Seeing her like that made me lose all my strength. I had to lean against the door. A man was in the room. A man sitting by the window with his back to the door. A bald man with his back to the door. I found this very odd and he didn't appear familiar. While I was staring at him over her naked shoulder, she banged the door shut. I heard her locking it. It was over. It had lost its savour . . . "

'She stopped and it was Carla's turn to begin murmuring her woes: "When her right leg began swelling, she didn't realise what it was at first, then the other followed. She took to wearing long skirts to hide them. Then her body and arms were attacked. She hid away in her room and only ventured out at night. The only one who was allowed to see her was an old Indian woman, believed by the islanders to be a witch. She is a herbalist, an excellent one. In fact, I've researched and marketed a number of her compounds. There is one especially which works wonders on the complexion. She tried to treat Maria with herbal compounds, but it was no use, no use at all . . . "

' "Carla, Carla don't torment yourself, put it out of your mind. Be like me and remember only her beauty, never her ugliness." And now it was Miss Tamada's turn to blubber and Carla's turn to comfort her. "Kumi also had turned ugly, but in her mind. She called me often, accusing me of being a spy, a traitor, an informer. Before, I had been concerned about her condition, now she only irritated me. I listened to what she said without responding . . . "

'But Carla did not listen for long, and broke in morbidly: "The old woman described to me how Maria's face became a giant pouch, a cow's udder which wobbled and swung every time she moved. The disease spread rapidly. Her two eyes became like buttons stuck on a football. Oh, Riyoko, it was terrible and sad." She began a wild wailing, and the roles were exchanged again.

'Miss Tamada administered physical relief, while murmuring: "Kumi too became repulsive to me. I dreaded, I became afraid of running into her on the street. Perhaps, I should have been closer to her. I thought I could feel Kumi's sweaty body on my skin and I loathed it . . . "

' "And Maria used to steal out at night. I imagine her on moonlit nights, her body wobbling and bouncing, a soggy ball of liquid down the slope. She was looking for a particular flower which grows on our mountain, a deadly flower and she used that . . . "

'Suddenly the attacks on my life returned to haunt me, and I couldn't hold myself in. "You mean, there is a poisonous flower growing on this mountain?"

' "Yes, a delicate white flower. And then she found that flower. It is somewhat rare. I can just imagine how, how tenderly she grasped it and brought it to her lips. I imagine her last thoughts. She thinks that there still might be a cure, then in a drop of dew clinging to that flower she sees the monstrosity she has become. Worse, she sees the reality of her fingers, great brown sausages struggling to hold the tender beauty of that flower—and unable to bear the sight she quickly pushes it through her great blubber lips. Oh, Maria, Maria, was it you, really you?" Again she breaks down and Miss Tamada holds her until she quiets.

'I look around for some drinks. They would buck all of us up, but there wasn't any and I feel the time is propitious to ask where they are.

' "There, there, Carla, there, there," Miss Tamada whispered. 'I know how it is. I do, I do. I remember seeing Kumi standing at the gate of my mother's house. She stood there alone, all alone. I must have looked nervous and startled, for she began to laugh. She wore torn jeans and a tight red T-shirt and looked haggard . . . She had gained some weight. Her lips and nails were painted red: I had never seen her before wearing such vivid lipstick. It made her lips appear coated with fresh blood. It, it frightened me, and it is the thing I remember most about her now . . . "

' "That old Indian amah told me a strange thing," Carla cut in, whispering her own tale of woe. "Maria was fond of pearls and I used to make her gifts of them. These islands were once surrounded by pearl-bearing oyster beds which my family plundered in amassing our fortune. They kept some pearls aside for a rainy day. Maria became my rainy day woman and I showered pearls on her. She seemed to get almost a sexual pleasure out of decking her brown beauty with them. Such a beautiful body and the pearls added lustre to it. It appears that when the disease gained a hold on her, it affected her mind. Her love of pearls became an obsession and she wore as many as she could. Then as the disease advanced, an extraordinary thing happened, the pearls began dying. They lost their lustre and darkened until they lay against her skin like tiny, round cinders. The amah swears this really happened and I have no reason to doubt her. It is what I remember about her now, here . . . " and her voice began to break . . . "her bloated body and her dead pearls. Oh God, oh God . . . "

' "There, there," Miss Tamada murmured. "I remember those bloody lips. I spoke to her trying not to look at them, telling myself to have a normal voice, a normal expression and normal gestures. But the more I tried, the more difficult it became. I knew that Kumi couldn't have failed to notice how I was acting. It began badly, continued badly, and degenerated into insults. I had loved her and now all that was left was an embarrassment which hurts when I think about it."

' "And as if her suffering wasn't enough," Carla exclaimed, her voice rising as she got some of her spirit back, "Maria wanted to be buried with her family in the main cemetery at Hermansburg. It was an overpowering desire. In fact, it is a custom here to have large family graves, and a family member not to be buried with the rest is considered a catastrophe. If a person is lost at sea as sometimes happens, an effigy of the loved one is buried in the grave. But in Maria's case, they refused to bury her in the family grave. What with her being a suicide and a huge, bloated corpse which bore no resemblance to the Maria they used to know, they actually disclaimed all knowledge of the corpse and left it to rot on the hillside. It was only when it had begun to decay and to stink to high heaven, that an Indian servant dug a hole and using a long pole pushed her corpse into it. Poor, poor Maria," she wailed out, but she still managed to keep her poise, so that I felt she was acting out a role. She exclaimed theatrically: "I feel like leaving this place; but no, I still feel that Maria has not bidden me farewell. I feel her presence." She looked around wildly, her gaze fastening on something behind me. Taken in by, by her performance, I darted a look behind. Nothing, of course.

' "God, go into the kitchen and get me a gin and lime and one for Miss Tamada too. God, I feel, feel so utterly devastated. I want to die," she wailed, her fist thudding into a silken cushion. The pug dog scuttled in alarm under the divan, and I left for the drinks as Carla dramatically flung her arms about Miss Tamada and cried: "Thank God, I have you, I really need you."

'I returned with the drinks to find both of them recovered except for a slight redness around the eyes. It had been an emotional scene, though now, on reflection, I consider it to have been somewhat far-fetched. I have a problem with those days. There is a kind of haze over them. It is almost as if I was drugged for the whole time I was there and suffered hallucinations. In fact, there was worse to come; but this occurred later . . .

'After we finished our drinks, Carla suggested that we stroll in the spacious garden which surrounded the bungalow on both sides and above and below. Miss Tamada particularly wanted to see it, as the garden had been landscaped by a Japanese who had been washed ashore during the Second World War and who had occupied his time with things Japanese.

'Miss Tamada, her past sorrows forgotten, that is if they had ever existed, hummed and hawed over the meandering paths and miniature plains, over the seemingly haphazard placement of the pine trees in which she found significant patterns hinting at the arrangement of the Imperial Gardens in Osaka, or Kyoto, or some such place. She was especially touched by the blue and white wisteria. Her excitement pushed away Carla's grief. We strolled along the main path which twisted and turned, ran back on itself and forked. One branch ran up the mountain; this Miss Tamada took as she wanted to get above the house and look down on the whole garden. The other branch, which Carla and I followed, descended to a huge cherry tree which seemed far too mature to date from the war.

'Carla stood against the dark trunk and as I stood staring at her beauty, all the unease caused by her relationship with Miss Tamada fled. If only the memory of the death of Maria had not clung to me, I might have tried to make love to her then and there. Instead, I admired her and the tree. Huge clusters of cherry blossoms hung from the austere darkness of the branches like masses of pinkish, white seashells spread over a beach of black volcanic sand, which I had been told existed on the island and had been marked for development, naturally by Kitsune Corporation, as the first tourist resort.

'How my mind and words go on. I assure you that I did not think those things then, at that precise moment. It was a sensual experience of a particular intensity, enhanced by the magic of that time between day and night. A cool sea-breeze brushed my skin as it went past to play with the tips of the branches. They bent gracefully in a rustle of cascading blossoms, then the thick, widespread boughs began themselves to sway with an easy grandeur as the day playfully fled the clutches of the pursuing tropic night. As I gazed, the tree-shape with the form of that beautiful woman blurred into a oneness; but the black of the tree trunk grew heavy and sombre. Carla herself was a splash of fading, golden light—now, see, it is that poetic streak I discovered in myself on the island. It lies, falsifies and beautifies. Too much harmony in this scene. Carla was too alive to be seen as merely part of the scenery, too much, I say, a woman of the world; at home in the boardroom as in the bedroom. Then, then, there is something else I admit. At the foot of the tree I caught the opening of some sort of cavern. Soft light gleamed. I started forward, then, then . . .

'This really happened. I swear it. Carla ripped herself from the dreary tree and the mouth of that cavern and ran to me. Her golden arms, pale in the gathering darkness, glided out and about my neck. She pulled my lips down to hers, gave me a hasty kiss, a mere touch, then drew back to ask: "Would you like to go and see one of the plantations tomorrow? You might find it of interest. You really need to know some of, some of what I would call, the transitional economy of the islands."

' "Tomorrow? Well, why not, but tomorrow is tomorrow," I exclaimed, pulling her to me.

' "How sweet you are, darling," she murmured.

'I buried my face in her hair. It held a strange animal odour which intoxicated me. I began backing her towards the cherry tree; but she resisted and murmured: "Not now, darling, not now, later. You'll enjoy the plantation, oh yes you will," she whispered in a tone which might have held promise or threat.

'I tried to kiss her again, but she pulled free just as Miss Tamada appeared to put a stop to my attempts at lovemaking. Carla, a swirl of silk, ran to Miss Tamada and linking their arms, they strolled back to the bungalow with me in tow. I tried to quash my disappointment; but my mood of despondency returned, and I looked forward to the relief of a gin and lime.'

SESSION NINE

'Well, what do you think of the, the idyllic scene in which I found myself? A lone man with two attractive female companions. Don't begin to envy me just yet, or ever, for those women were not your true-blue Aussie sheilas at all. To put it mildly, they were somewhat perverse. The garden scene had been nice, and we went back to the bungalow where thankfully Miss Tamada made herself scarce. Carla took my hand and led me into a room hung with peach-coloured silk behind which lights glowed softly. She was one for cloth and draperies, and for couches heaped with cushions. Almost every room in the bungalow had one. Now she slipped down on it, pulled me down beside her, then stroked my forehead with her electric touch. At last, I thought, I was to be alone with her. But she was up almost at once and left to slip into something more comfortable. This meant a kimono, silk of course, and one which reflected her eyes and skin colouring. She entered fastening the sash about her waist, then threw me a dark silk kimono. I was expected to put it on, and in front of her. I managed to do this and she left me on the couch while she fussed about a low table. It was then Miss Tamada came trotting in clad in a fresh kimono; but one which was more elaborate. She also had a huge wig on her head and her face was made up stark white. Her feral eyes gleamed out at me. She carried some tiny jugs of saki and tinier cups. She motioned Carla to the table, shot a glance at me, then left.

' "Tonight's the night for Riyoko's gourmet special," Carla smiled.

' "Oh," I replied, thinking it might be some Jap delicacy, or other. We had some pretty good Japanese restaurants on the Gold Coast, and naturally I had been in more than one or two. What I didn't like was raw fish. It wasn't the taste so much as the, the texture of the damn stuff. I liked my fish and chips as did all Aussies, but well, my fish had to be at least half-done, if not coated in batter and deep-fried. Carla smiled at me as I muttered: "Not that raw fish, I hope?"

' "No, Riyoko has been dying to try our Fuju fish. If it is as good as I think it is, it'll be a plus for our island. The Japanese love it. You know they have a saying, only a fool eats Fuju, and only a fool doesn't eat Fuju. So, perhaps you'll lose out both ways."

'It seemed that Carla was wrong for Riyoko came back carrying a steaming pot in which pieces of cooked fish were floating. I glanced at her and asked: "Is this the famous Fuju?" Then I added facetiously: "The fish and chips of Japan."

'Miss Tamada refused to be drawn into levity. In all ways she seemed as dour as the Scottish skipper of the *Tui-tui*. She carefully set the dish on the table, placed chopsticks and small bowls in front of us and said: "*Chiru!*"

' "And what is that?" I asked.

' "The Japanese equivalent of fish stew," she replied, and I remembered that the skipper also had had a dry sense of humour.

' "But a special one," Carla laughed, "and who'll be the first to try it? They say the first one who does takes her life in her hands."

' "Just a fish stew," I exclaimed. "Well, if someone has to be the first, I shall."

'Both of them watched me seriously. Ignoring the chopsticks, I poured some of the broth and fish pieces into a bowl, and demanded a spoon. Carla sighed and Miss Tamada trotted off to the kitchen to return with one. Under their eyes, I spooned the soup down. It hardly had any taste. Not much taste at all. The women continued to watch me.

' "Well," Carla said, "I'll sample a piece." She took up a pair of chopsticks, broke them apart and daintily picked up a piece of fish. She held it in front of her face. I suddenly gave a gasp, which stopped her from completing her action. My mouth began tingling and I tried to drag in a breath through my contracting throat. Suddenly a spasm went through my body.

' "You, you," I managed to whisper at the Japanese woman, then I felt myself sliding off to one side. Carla caught my body and stretched it out on the floor. I tried to move and couldn't. Paralysed. Panic. I couldn't do a thing, couldn't move a muscle. But my mind was as clear as a bell.

' "Riyoko," Carla exclaimed, bending over me, "I believe your *chiru* has claimed a victim."

'I stared up at her face, marvelling at the redness of the lips uttering those words and at those emerald eyes glinting with specks of gold. I was dying. I knew it; but I couldn't do a thing about it. They had got me.

'Another face, a white mask with glittering eyes came to bend over me. "Sometimes it happens like this. *Chiru* should be respected, not gulped down. It must be savoured. Too bad. The toxin drains from the flesh into the broth. It should not be drunk; but a fool and his life are quickly parted."

'In my field of vision, she calmly took the chopsticks from Carla's hand and ate the piece of fish. "It is tangy, not as good as Japanese; but, ah, there is the tingling of the lips you get from this fish when it is properly prepared. There it is on my tongue. Only a slight numbness. Have a piece," and she extended a morsel at the end of her chopsticks to Carla. I watched the fish disappear between her ruby lips. I wished to shout that it was poisoned, but could not move my lips.

Carla chewed gently, then said, "Yes, I see what you mean."

' "A little saki will bring out the full flavour," Riyoko added.

'Leaving me on the floor, they sipped on their tiny cups of saki and chewed on the morsels of fish. I tried to feel anger at this callous treatment, but my mind refused to accept it. Now I knew that their plot had succeeded and I was dying. I wondered what they would do with my body. It was then that Carla bent over me again. I stared into that lovely face slightly flushed from the alcohol. It calmly regarded me for a moment, then her face came down close to mine and her hand went to my chest. "You know, Riyoko, he isn't breathing at all. We must do something. We can't leave him here all night. I know how poisonous puffer fish can be; but, well, do we sling him into a spare room and leave him there? Can he be revived?"

'The Japanese woman knelt beside her. I watched her arm slip around Carla's waist, although watched wasn't the proper word. My eyes too were paralysed and I saw what was only in my narrow field of vision.

' "Sometimes, people recover quickly, sometimes they do not," Miss Tamada stated as if, as if it was simply a minor business matter. "They say that it is like a living death. The body is paralysed and the mind remains clear. There is a ceremony which the Ainu, the original people of Japan, have, except that the shaman who does the ceremony is said to own the soul of the person he saves, and who wants to own this soul? My Australian friend, the Aborigine man, was most interested in the Ainu and their ceremonies. They were most interested in him too. He and I are very good friends and when he came to Japan . . . "

' "Riyoko, I know him too. I wonder how he is getting on. It is some time since I saw him. He put me onto a most interesting natural remedy, though very, very expensive. It is a honey, extracted from what they call the honey ant and it appears to retard aging. Of course, it is still undergoing research, but the results are more than good. In fact, excellent. I meant to look him up in Australia, but the Prime Minister told me that he was on a most sensitive mission and that I might run across him sooner than I expected."

' "He is like that. He appears when you least expect him . . . But at the moment we are concerned with this person lying in front of us. You know, sometimes they only appear dead. I have heard that people have been buried alive."

'Inwardly I shuddered. I struggled to make them aware that I was alive. Paralysed yes, but alive. Already, I could feel the grave closing over me. I struggled, but could do nothing. Was I doomed to a fate worse than death?

' "Do you think that he is alive?" Carla asked. "He doesn't look it. Perhaps, if only you knew that ceremony. It should be quite amusing and I might take the ownership of this soul upon myself. After all, if you own a car, you can leave it in the garage for years, if you want to. Ownership does not suggest responsibility, does it?"

' "Not to the person who is the owner, but perhaps to the person who is owned," Miss Tamada replied gravely.

' "Do, do you, recall how the ceremony went?" Carla asked, somewhat breathlessly. She bent over my face again, her green eyes gravely regarding it. She took a pinch of my cheek between thumb and forefinger and nipped. At least, I think she did, for I had no feeling or response. "Well," she again asked the Japanese woman, "do you know it?"

' "Maybe, for some of my family were double-lived ones, were shamans, and there is the matter of the fox. That will make a connection. There are also certain things I need, a drum, a wooden wand, a fox skull and some other things."

' "Well, a drum is easy to obtain, but I don't know about the other things. You said shamans. My family are great collectors and I believe there are ritual objects, skulls and things, from this island and others. My grandfather was an avid collector of such curiosities. Come on, let's go and check over his collection."

'They ran off like, like two schoolgirls, leaving me to my misery, or rather to my clear consciousness of the room. My field of vision held the table and part of the ceiling; my ears collected sounds of crickets, cicadas, the call of a night bird, the brushing of wind against the walls, the sound of a door being opened, the female voice, sounds of Carla and Miss Tamada.

'They were gone for too long. I lay there in a blue funk. I could see myself in a coffin, the lid being screwed down, the darkness, the thud of earth on the wood. I wanted to be mad, I wanted to cry out; but all I was a clear consciousness without the ability to do a thing.

'The women came back into the room, seeming light-footed

and eager. They passed through my field of vision and I saw that they had found what they had been seeking. I also saw that they were naked, except for strange ornaments of bone, teeth and dull stones. Necklaces, bracelets, anklets and what have you. Miss Tamada put other things on the low table, collected the remains of, of the repast and left the room again. Carla looked at me, then tapped on the drum while she waited. She grew impatient and came to me. She felt my forehead for some reason, then twisted my head so that my field of vision now swept across the table and room. "I wonder if there are any dances," she murmured to herself, and attempted a few steps.

' "No dances," Miss Tamada said, entering the room with a hibachi stove from which flames flickered. She placed it on the table, took up the drum then warmed it over the fire. She then picked up what looked suspiciously like a human femur and gave the drum a few whacks, heated the skin some more, then set up a fast, circular rhythm. "Here you try it," she said to Carla. She did so and the drum rattled out. "Just let it come naturally like that," Miss Tamada advised her. "The drum will talk to you, and you'll go along with it."

'Carla brought the drum and sat next to my head. She began beating out the rhythm. The Japanese woman took up a carved stick, frowned at it, then passed it over the fire. She tapped it on the ground a few times and muttered something. She picked up a skull of some animal and warmed that too. It was filled with small bones. She spilt these out on the table-top, then scooped them up again. She waved and warmed the wand, while flinging handfuls of stuff into the fire. Some caused the flames to leap; others caused them to smoulder; still others raised a thick cloud of smoke. Finally she passed the skull and then the wand through the fire for a last time, then came towards me. Carla increased the tempo. Miss Tamada carried the skull in one hand and the wand in the other. She passed the skull over my body; then gave a loud "Lha-ha-ha-ha-ha" and began striking me with the wand starting at my feet. I felt nothing; but I heard what seemed to be some animal alight on the roof and scrabble around up there. The Japanese woman took the wand back to the fire and flung it down on the table. She turned and her face looked angry and fierce. She stalked towards me, grabbed the drum from in front of Carla and beat out a stronger rhythm. She flung the drum back at her, then returned to the table. She picked up something and turned. It was a snake. She flung it towards my head. I saw its mouth gape, heard it say, "Pish, pish."

'It was then that my eyes moved and opened wide. I felt my eyeballs stick right out of their sockets. Miss Tamada turned. She held a spear in her hand. She came towards me and I closed my eyes.

'The drum beat faster and faster, then stopped. I could hear the panting of the two women, and the scrape of flesh on flesh as a wave of darkness and feeling began at the soles of my feet and moved upwards through my body. Thankfully, I slid into, let that darkness blacken my consciousness.

SESSION TEN

'I think, I think that you are beginning to doubt the veracity of my statements. You feel, though you do not state, and your, your questions seek to elicit what you may term the "truth". But I query the whole concept of "truth" and as for reality, the so-called getting to the heart of that matter, well, often the heart of the matter is vastly different from the skin of the subject. You hesitate; more than once I have seen your finger hover over the off-button. You wish to wipe me from your narrative. You wonder what my narration has to do with the one and only Dr Watson Holmes Jackamara. You think all these things, and yet you persist as I persisted in that infernal situation in which I found myself. Do you wish me to declare that I truly died, was deliberately poisoned by that fiend masquerading as a businesswoman? I know that you hide a smile of derision; but I did suffer a poisoning which almost did me in and I had to put up with an absurd ritual which worked on my mind. I have heard of certain techniques of brainwashing. Now you openly smirk. Perhaps I should mention drugs? Your smirk becomes a grin. Well, mate, the world is filled with drugs and with those employing them on innocent people such as myself; but, mind you, I am not, cannot make any accusations. In this climate, it is impossible. My enemies are powerful, my friends non-existent, and I? You wish me to continue my narrative? I shall, I shall.

'The next morning I came to in that peach-coloured room with the light streaming through the windows. Nothing remained to remind me of the events of the night, except a lassitude which gripped my limbs and a numbness of mind which almost refused me thought. I lay there in my weakness and had to endure the arrival of the two women who were in the best of spirits. They declared that I had had an adverse reaction to the fish, that the saki had proved too strong for my constitution, that I had passed out and they had left me here to sleep it off. They said this last sentence with smiles of complicity into which I frowned. Miss Tamada wrinkled her nose at me, then left, and Carla urged me to shower, get dressed and have some breakfast. "You'll feel heaps better," she declared, "and the journey to the plantations will give you a new lease of life."

'I shuddered at this; but she, not to be denied, bustled me into the bathroom and left me there. The shower did some good and the donning of a new pair of shorts, a bush shirt and long socks and shoes did restore me to some degree of normality. I almost could imagine myself back on the Coast and ready to see a client. I went to the dining room and was served coffee and rolls. This was all that I could face; that is until I smelt the aroma of bacon and eggs. I needed an Aussie breakfast and soon was tucking into one. I had recovered to all intents and purposes and even looked forward to seeing some of the island, casting my eye over the real estate as it were.

'We were late in starting and were driven around the base of the mountain and through a jungle which already had the aspect of a tended national park which I liked, for who needs the scruffiness of the natural? This changed, however, when we swung off the road along a dirt track which led through the rainforest to the head of a path threading its way through the dank growth. I hung back as the women got out. The driver looked back at me.

' "Come on," Carla called. "It's only about a kilometre and well worth the walk. Bring the hamper," she ordered the driver, and then without waiting for me to make up my mind, hurried off with Miss Tamada. The driver smiled at me ruefully, then went to the boot to get the munchies. I walked after the females and found myself plodding through mushy ground and edging along sunken logs which formed the path. The trees dripped moisture on me and the undergrowth bristled with huge flowers and on one of them sat a huge green frog which croaked at me. I didn't like the walk at all. It was like pressing through a nightmarish tunnel and who knew what lurked in wait for me; then, then, there had been those incidents and this was a better place than most for the final and fatal accident. A body lying at the side of the path would dissolve into mush within days, and worse now the path was hugging the side of a gully at the bottom of which, through a tangle of wrecked logs and vile undergrowth, I could catch a glimpse of a stream and hear its rush.

'At last, I came down and out on the bank of the stream. Boulders and rocks formed a rough platform and there the women were. They saw me and waved, then rushed off along another path. I sat down on the rocks and stared at the rushing water. It was a pleasant spot, but there was an air of foreboding hanging over it. I stared at the rancid pool which had collected all the debris which rushed down a waterfall. The water flowed over a steep slope, then fell over a short cliff into the pool. I stared up and saw Carla waving to me from the top. I watched her as she made her way across the lip of the waterfall to the opposite bank. She stopped and I thought she might attempt to clamber down; but she made her way back and disappeared. I looked at the spot and could see the heads of the bamboo grove we had come especially to see. It was then that the driver came up lugging the hamper and began preparing morning tea. He was ready to hand the two women an ice-cold drink of mineral water when they emerged from the path. I smiled a surly "hello" and turned to the pool. I needed a cold beer to get my mind off things, but there wasn't any. I consoled myself with a cup of tea, then bit into sandwiches which had a filling of some sort of expensive liverwurst. It tasted raw and brought up the events of the previous night. I felt quite sick and went and scrambled over the rocks to stare down into the water. I scooped some up and was about to drink it, when I felt Carla grab my shoulder as she leapt onto my small rock. I almost overbalanced and turned to her to remonstrate, but just like a woman she got out the first word: "See that black rock there, that big one poking out of the bank beside the waterfall. There is an old native legend connected with it . . . "

' "I know, I know?" I exclaimed irritably, "one of your forebears also was a collector of native legends."

' "Why, how did you know?" she replied, sweetly. "But not a man, a woman, and naturally she concentrated on the folklore of women. In fact, she constructed the original building where my bungalow now stands. Behind it, I might show it to you, if you want to see it, is a spring where this particular mythic female being likes to visit. She roams from here to there, or rather flies. Sometimes, you can see her as a light in the sky. Naturally I have seen it, then when she arrives here she becomes, or enters, into that rock. I'm not sure about that part, nor was my grandmother. She has another body too. Tall and slim with long flowing hair, beautiful slender hands and long finger nails."

' "A perfect description of you," I exclaimed, my mind flitting to Jackamara's story and then to the Japanese woman's tales. To tell the truth, I was getting pretty tired of these female whimsies. They belonged to that New Age junk which I had read about in newspapers, and heard from aging and gushing women at parties. Still, it was such fancies that lurked behind the runaway success of the Sas shops, and who was I to deride superstitions when there was a buck to be made from them?'

' "In fact I've named one of my lines after her. It is quite popular too . . . "

' "Indeed," I muttered, "and naturally you have a Foxy line and a Shaman perfume too."

' "Why," she exclaimed, "so you have been into one of my shops, but, I suspect only from curiosity, or perhaps dragged in by a woman friend. Did she select Foxee? It couldn't have been Shaman, for that's a men's line of toiletries. 'For the man with a mind for mystic views', and naturally, the mystic vision is female. In fact, and she turned sad, Maria modelled for the ad."

' "Of course," I replied, "of course."

'In a huff, I turned my back on her and stared at the boulder which contained or was the so-called spirit. It was just a roundish rock with the shape of a breast, and hence the identification of boulder with female. It was just then that Carla jumped from the rock on which we were perched. It shifted slightly and I felt myself moving forward. My arms waved frantically and then I was floundering in the water and there she was laughing down at me. "You shouldn't swim here," she said, "for that spirit tempts men into the pool and drowns them."

' "Oh bosh," I exclaimed, dragging myself from the water which I thought smelled like women's pee.

'I scrambled to the bank and found a deserted spot where I could strip, wring out my clothes and spread them to dry. I was sick and tired of female company. I lay back and enjoyed the sun sprinkling its maleness on the rocks. How quiet it was without them.

'A half-hour later, the driver came to inform me that they were ready to continue. I pulled on my damp clothing and walked back with him to the vehicle. I got into the front seat, excusing myself because of my wet clothing. I wished to be alone with my thoughts; but Carla's voice came to me from the back seat. At least this time she kept to business facts and not silly superstitions.

' "You'll be surprised at our plantations. We are well ordered and efficient. We have to be, or go under, especially now when we are about to become an independent nation. At one time we used to grow bananas for the New Zealand market; that fell apart and we tried sugarcane which came to a sticky end. Now we have changed over to aromatic and medical oils. You would be surprised how large a market there are for them, and then we have our shops which take most of our production. Vertical integration means that we can produce a product of certified purity. The old man is a whiz at picking the right crop at the right time, and we have been interested in exotic oils for centuries. Moreover he's a great scientist, though unorthodox, and then we have our research and development experts. You'd be surprised at the extent of our holdings."

' "Perhaps," I couldn't help gloating, "but I faxed my

broker to buy shares in the Sas holding company."

' "Sorry, darling," she exclaimed, "but they're tightly controlled. They're worth their weight in gold."

'This piece of information made it urgent that I get to my broker and get my money working for me. Little did I know then, that after he found that Sas was not available, he had kept the shares I had urged him to sell with the result that now I had lost out again. But this is later. Now, I merely wondered what to buy.

'We reached the flat coastal plain and passed through the ordered rows of plantation crops. What they were, I did not know, though perhaps I should have made it my business. The aloe vera herb had made me a small but tidy profit before the bottom fell out of the scheme. These were not aloe vera. They were small, evenly spaced plants with thick leaves of green and had been planted for some time. They most likely yielded some oil or other. I glanced back at Carla to ask her; but she seemed to have withdrawn into herself. She sat away from Miss Tamada, huddled in the corner of the seat as if pondering over something. Most likely it had to do with business, and how she could extend her holdings, or she may even have been thinking that by inviting the Kitsune Corporation in she was effectively losing control of her island. I wondered if she had had much experience with dealing with Japanese firms. We in Queensland had. The main object was to keep a controlling interest while using their money and expertise. Perhaps it would be to my advantage if I got her away from Miss Tamada and advised her. In fact, I could become her adviser and negotiate for her.

'I turned and looked at her and then at Miss Tamada. The Japanese woman's eyes met mine. She knew of my business dealings and she would stymie my plans, or would she? There is more than one way to pluck a chook and I knew those other ways.

'After an hour of steady driving, we turned our backs on the mountain and drove towards what must be the edge of the land. We turned down an avenue between rows of tall coconut palms which led to a stately building. A surprise on this island of surprises. It was not a low, rambling bungalow, but a tall, creamy two-storey mansion with a colonnaded front which made me think of the American South, or rather the American South of *Gone with the Wind*, for I had never been away from LA or New York.

'Carla broke her moody silence to explain: 'A great-grandfather is responsible for this. He went to America and latched onto the gracious plantation life there. He had this house built by black craftsmen he imported from Louisiana, and so there it stands a monument to him and his particular needs and those of my great-grandmama too. Only a manager lives there now, but he is part of the monument. It seems that great-grandmama was quite taken with one of the craftsmen and so was great-grandpapa for he never did complain; though the British part of our family did. They couldn't stick it that an American, especially a black one, might join our blood line; but it did have a positive result as you'll see for yourself. Maynard Brookes is quite a man.''

'I nodded politely into the rear-vision mirror—through which I was watching Carla's suddenly animated face as she affected an American southern accent. She was so beautiful and a fine example of so-called mixed breeding. I was all for this, especially as I was the result of Irish, English, German and Italian stock myself and another fine example of the mixing of the races. Don't smile; besides, what really interested me was how I might turn my acquaintanceship with this remarkable though somewhat flaky woman and family to my account. I knew that I had to remain alert and ready to seize the main chance when it came. And it would come, for with independence there would be an inflow of Australian aid and if I had an "in" to the ruling family of the island, or failing them the Opposition, I would be in the right place at the right time. The good old Prime Minister, bless his heart, had steered me towards a good thing, and I mentally thanked him as we pulled up in front of the mansion.

'My faith in humanity restored, as soon as the vehicle

stopped I hopped out to open Carla's door for her. Side by side, almost a couple (I ignored Miss Tamada) we turned to face that colonnaded front. I let myself feel that I was beginning a scene in *Gone with the Wind*. I was escorting Scarlet home and I expected a uniformed black butler to descend upon us. Such are dreams made of. "The land behind slopes to the cliff edge. You get a spectacular view from there. I'll take you after we meet Maynard. Ah, there he is now," Carla said.

'No uniformed black butler, but a tall, broad-shouldered, slim-waisted movie star in a rumpled safari suit came striding around the corner of the building. He stopped in midstride as he caught sight of Carla. His handsome face glowed as he strode towards her and clasped her in his manly arms. His glance flickered across me and then lingered on Miss Tamada. I stood there feeling clumsy and out of place. Only a bit player in this movie; but hasn't that always been my fate? . . .

' "Maynard Brookes, the Manager of Mariian Plantation," Carla said, swinging him around so that he faced me, then swinging him around again so that he faced Miss Tamada. Brookes broke away from Carla and took a long stride to the Japanese woman. She positively simpered, then wrinkled up her nose and laughed. He held her hand for a long instant before reluctantly letting it fall as he turned to me.

' "Pleased to meet you," I said, extending my hand. He picked it up and dropped it. He turned and clapped his hands. A young girl ran from the house front. He told her to bring us cold drinks as if he was asking her to do him a favour. She smiled and ran to do his bidding. He took Carla's and Riyoko's arms and guided them into the cool interior of the mansion. Slowly, I followed.

' "Heck of a place to air-condition," Brookes told Carla, releasing the arm of Miss Tamada to sweep his hand around the wide hall and the broad staircase. "In the old man's day, all this meant gracious living and coolness from the high ceilings. I suppose it didn't work then and it doesn't work now. It's only made our job more complicated. You should see the size of the air-conditioning unit we had to get. The power drain on our generators will be enormous; but soon we'll have our powerhouse" . . . and he turned to Miss Tamada with a smile.

'Miss Tamada had left her computer in the car, or thought she had; but the driver had brought in the luggage and she quickly had the machine up and running and flashing diagrams and statistics at him.

' "Well, Kitsune Corporation is certainly efficient, and such an electricity supply and network will cater for all our expansion plans for the next decade. But until it is up and running, our generators must do the job. We don't need these ceiling fans anymore; but I've left them up for that tropical island feel. People expect, not only Sadie Thompson, but slow-moving fans even if the joint is fully air-conditioned. Well, we won't cheat our guests, shall we?"

'Already I disliked this conceited ass, and who the hell was Sadie Thompson? If she was tropical, how come I had never heard of her? And as for slow-moving fans, we had more than enough of them in the cheaper places along the Gold Coast. Who needed them with air-conditioning? I watched him caressing Carla's arm and disliked him all the more, especially that deep voice he affected.

' "Since you've been away, there's been some changes. I expect that you're dying to see them. I'll take you and our colleague around a little later."

'I perked up when he mentioned "colleague", but it was directed at the Japanese woman. I stood there fuming as both women basked in his film star good looks and affectations. They smiled too much and stood too close. The bloke was lapping it up. I cursed Carla for putting me in this position, especially when she flashed a look of green fire at me with a golden glint of amusement in it. Her warped sense of humour I could do without.

'The girl entered with an iced jug filled with a concoction of rum-based punch, a speciality of the island and naturally invented by one of their ancient relatives. They sipped their glasses and I gulped mine down. At last alcohol and I had been simmering since the ducking I had taken in that confounded pool, and the simmering had reached boiling point with the bloke's treatment and the women's obvious enjoyment of his company. After the fourth drink, I found the jug empty, but I was decidedly mellow. Brookes looked at my empty glass and ordered another jug. He turned to the women and said something. They laughed, then his words became audible as he asked Carla if she wanted to see the improvements. She agreed eagerly, exchanged a glance with Miss Tamada, then gave a flash of green fire in my general direction and said: "You won't mind, will you darling, if we go off for a little while? This is going to be our future state guesthouse, and the furnishings are on their way now. Maynard may be able to handle generators and things, but I doubt if he is the sort to go in for interior decorating."

'I did not share in her laughter. "Go right ahead, don't mind me," I muttered grumpily. "I'll have another drink, then find something to do. Mind if I have a look outside? I haven't been on a plantation for some time. That was when I was investing in macadamias in northern New South Wales. I would like to see the set-up here and who knows what opportunities I might find," I hinted—a good way of doing business when you supposedly weren't doing business.

' "Yes, yes, occupy yourself as best you can, my sweet. It'll be only for a little while; but I must warn you that Maynard is landscaping a garden about the mansion and you won't see any of our cash crops. The workers' quarters are a kilometre away. Not because we don't want them near; but because we are anxious to preserve the pretty little Neo-Polynesian village in which they live."

'The girl returned with another jug of the iced punch and I quickly poured myself a drink. The others decided to have another too, and this left me time for another one, then two. I was fair staggering when at last Maynard pushed me through a side door and pointed down a garden path. I lurched, recovered my balance, then staggered off determined to act out my role as an Australian agent. Maybe I could find out something and revenge myself on all of them.

'The Neo-Polynesian village was as much a joke, or as sad as, any Aboriginal settlement. I suppose that it had been Carla's idea of a joke. Certainly there were thatched huts, but these were dilapidated and clustered about a tin shed. I looked for the chapel and then for the mission bungalow, but these did not exist. I felt flushed and hot as I staggered into the shed, blinked in the sudden gloom, then lurched as a voice said: "Elias Faitoaga." A brown oversized bloke stuck out his hand, crushed my fingers, and while I was attempting to straighten them, called to his mate, Adaboaga, who was bent over a lathe, or some such machinery which you find in machine shops. Adaboaga switched off the machine and came erect. I saw a familiar black face. He winked at me, then put a finger to his lips. I was dumbfounded. My mouth gaped like a fish; the euphoric state induced by the rum punch vanished, for I recognised that face. I was in the presence of Detective Inspector Watson Holmes Jackamara!

'Ah, now I have your attention. You thought that I was waffling on, but I was leading up to this. There he was in the, in the camp of the enemy and perfectly at home in it. Here I was, there I was a guest with the ruling family of the island and an agent of the Australian Government and I had at last met my contact. "So, you're really an Aussie," he said with a grin of complicity. He crossed his arms across his naked chest.

"He may well be," his mate, Elias, said with a smile, setting his back against a workbench and eyeing me. "We heard that you were on our island, but never thought we might contact you."

' "Yes," agreed Adaboaga, Detective Inspector Watson Holmes Jackamara in disguise. "We don't get that many free visitors on our islands. We used to get contract gangs from Kiwiland, but not anymore. Now it's those little yellow fellows they call Koreans. Not a word of English amongst them. They jabber on and on in their lingo and we can't catch a word. Just visiting the place, are you?"

'Elias threw back his huge head and gave a huge laugh.

Jackamara warned me to be silent. He seemed privy to my mission; but then if he was, why had Jackamara warned me not to reveal his true identity? I was on the horns of a dilemma. I prided myself on being a good judge of men and decided to reveal my mission; but first, I decided on a test. I switched to the subject of their coming independence.

' "Yeah," Elias boomed, "we get our independence. But what then?" he spluttered. "Can we stand up to those who think they are above us? They have always been there and it is even written down as hard fact in our scriptures. Scripture does not lie. It is something we must endure, my Aussie friend."

'I shrugged at such rubbish from a giant of a man who should have been ready to seize his freedom in both great hands and give it a vigorous shake. Jackamara gave me a wink again, then snapped: "We have to stand up to those white men and afakasi. Stand up and tell them that these islands are ours. When the day of freedom dawns, it shall be we who will be forming our own government."

'Elias boomed with delight at such radical talk. "You listen to that radio of yours too much, boy. All them words suck up your brains. You can't read a single word of scripture, yet you think that you know all there is to know. What do you think, eh, you going to be president, or something like that when you can't read a single word?"

'His laughter sounded like thunder shaking the roof: "And you think this Aussie will help you? He is a guest of them that control our lives. There is a rumour that he is a government man come to see us get our independence; but is he when he eats and lives with them? Well, ask his help, boy. Go to it, take him up to the top of the ridge, let him meet Lataoga, the one who declares that he is the leader of all the people on these islands. Yes, take him to that one. Let him see for himself. They, these are all the same. Let them fight and battle one another until that great day comes, as foretold in the scriptures, when He shall come to rid us of all enslavement."

' "It is my intention to take him," declared Jackamara. He winked at me and I nodded. "See, he agrees to come and judge for himself. Our future lies with Lataoga who wishes to talk for all of us, not just a single clan. Times are changing, our islands are changing, and we must change with them. I need no book to see, to feel these changes; but if I must learn to read, I shall, but it will not be to read that book you make so much of." He scowled at Elias who boomed at him his great laugh which suddenly set Jackamara to laughing also.

'It was then that I realised that there was a method in their quarrelling, that it was a device by Jackamara to pass on information to me and also not to get me to commit myself to one side or the other as yet. Also and slyly, almost as if the other had suggested it, he had arranged for me to meet the leader of the independence movement, Lataoga.

'Suddenly I found myself sharing in their laughter. This was my chance to bypass Carla and her family and align myself with what appeared to be a viable Opposition. At last my mission was under way. Good, I could use another one of those rum punches.'

SESSION ELEVEN

'After the trip and the events of the day I found it easy to make excuses to go to my room early. The others weren't too chirpy either and they were going to make it an early night. I set my wristwatch alarm for 9.30 pm so that I could have a couple of hours of sleep, for I knew that my night would be a long one. On hearing the alarm I got up, had a shower, pulled on my now dry things and trying not to make any noise eased into the corridor. A night lamp dully gleamed and helped me along. I reached Carla's room and hesitated as I heard voices, a male and two females. I slipped past, down the staircase and to the side door I had used that afternoon. I unbolted it and went through. With luck, I would be back before daybreak and no one would be the wiser. Outside, the moon was almost full and the stars were blazing. The grounds were illuminated by an intense silvery light which I had not seen before, not even in Queensland, the state with the mostest. I walked to the workshop where Jackamara had promised to wait for me.

'Jackamara the Aborigine, and possibly the ASIO agent as well, was in his primitive element. I tried to find the Queensland policeman in the black man and couldn't. I tried to question him, but he put his finger to his lips and glided away. Perforce I was obliged to follow. We hurried through the straight rows of the plantation and away from the mansion and into the rainforest. He took me along a winding jungle track leading up and up. We were going towards the central mountain of the island. Now we were halfway up and near the edge of a deep gorge. Before going on Jackamara squatted to catch his breath beside a lump of earth the size of a small house. I looked back the way we had come. Under the intense moon and starlight, every object stood out as distinct as on a cloudy day, though the shadows were abrupt and intangible, distortions from the norm.

'The mansion was a dark bulk in which a few orange lights glowed. I thought of Maynard and Carla together and glowed with jealousy. Around that centre of jealousy, lesser straight-edged shapes were sheds. I saw gleams of red which I took to be the dying embers of cooking fires. Beyond the mansion, the dark of the earth was replaced by the twinkling silver sea. I could not make out the cliff edge from where I was, but the ocean waters moved under my eyes like some, some mottled serpent restlessly itching with unknown desires.

'Jackamara suddenly snorted, got up and went to the path where it descended at right angles into the gorge. He pulled out a torch and flashed it down three times. An answering light winked up. We began moving along the track. I skinned my ankle as I stepped on a patch of solid earth which was not there. The moonlight was deceptive. I hurried after him and tapped him on the shoulder. I asked him to slow down, then questioned if such melodramatics were necessary and whether there wasn't a shorter and easier route to where we were bound. He snorted at me and said, if you could believe it, that he had heard over The Voice of America that vigilance was the eternal price of freedom. I almost snarled at this. This man after all was an Australian and I suppose some of our leaders, or thinkers, had said much the same thing, but better. I lurched again and had to watch my feet. We were at the bottom of the gorge where the moon and stars did not penetrate.

' "Can't you slow down a bit?" I gasped to my guide; but in reply he quickened his pace. I hobbled after him enduring the painful throbbing of my ankle. "Not used to mountain climbing, got no head for heights, or bottoms," I muttered, trying a touch of humour. In answer, Jackamara slowed, then suddenly shot out a hand. I stopped and shuddered. The darkness at the bottom of the gorge had effectively camouflaged a narrow crevasse into which, but for his restraining hand, I would have tumbled. I leapt back from the crumbling edge and cursed myself for allowing myself to be inveigled into making such a trip. I should have stayed in the mansion, for

after my sleep, I could have made a night of it, that is if any
of the others were willing to. There was that little servant girl,
and I sighed.

' "Soon be there," my guide said as he led me to one side
where a log balanced across the crevasse. I ran over it. If I was
going to fall, I was going to fall. He watched, I could feel
his eyes, then turned away with a grunt. The gorge petered
out, and I took a glance at the luminescent face of my watch.
We had been going for three hours. It was just after one, and
I hoped that we wouldn't spend much time at the camp, or
whatever was our destination, for I really wanted to be home
and housed before daybreak. I may have wanted to be one up
on Carla, that infernal Japanese woman, and that pretty bloke,
but I did not want to burn my boats to do this.

'The track now wormed its way through thick rainforest.
Tall trees shut out much of the light and the way was
treacherous. So much so that Jackamara had to hack away with
a machete in places. This made me think that this was not
the main track to where we were going and that I was being
deliberately taken to the objective by a roundabout route. I
couldn't understand the need for this—for there was only one
mountain on the island and with a pair of good binoculars,
the gorge most likely would be visible from the mansion, or
even Carla's bungalow. Still, they must have a reason and who
was I to question their reasons. I let it go at that, too occupied
with pushing my way through the dense foliage. "How much
further?" I grunted.

' "Not far, almost there."

'Then I had the feeling that I was being watched, that eyes
were following my every step. This feeling strengthened as the
trees began to thin and the moonlight to streak in. I glimpsed
a narrow, rushing stream which made a moaning sound, and
it made me think of that female spirit, or thing, or rock, which
lived in that pool and which travelled from pool to spring.
For all I knew, this stream eventually fell into that pool. For
all I knew, the bungalow was not that far away. I found myself
wondering about the sadness, the impetus that drove that

woman spirit. Trapped, travelling eternally from pool to spring, from spring to pool and back and forth again and again. I looked up in the sky and back the way we had come. There was a will-o'-the-wisp following along behind. I thought of Miss Tamada's foxfire, and then of the *Gyinggi* woman and her connection with such lights. I stared back and it came charging in towards me. I felt my hair crackle and my skin burn. I thought of that *Kwinkan* and the flesh melting from his bones. I felt the sweat dripping from my body, dripping as if my flesh was dripping away. I shuddered and rushed to put myself between Jackamara and the light. I tripped and fell. He helped me up and I mentioned the light. He smiled and said that they were often seen on the mountain and seemed undisturbed. I pulled myself together and then thought of Carla and Brookes together. I hated them, I hated them. I was out here to get revenge. I stared down the track wildly. No light, just shadows, and then one of those shadows moved. I recoiled and meant to run; but Jackamara had one strong hand on my arm. He turned and stopped. I had to stop with him. I had to wait, and for what? Carla, that spirit woman, that *Gyinggi* woman. I thought I glimpsed a fox slinking across a patch of moonlight. I had been followed. They were on to me; out to get me. I wouldn't survive. I had been set up; but no, no, I knew Jackamara was here beside me, an agent of the Australian Government. I pushed superstitious forebodings aside and concentrated desperately on mine, on our mission. I was not alone and I had the strong arm of the Queensland law alongside me.

' "And who is that with you?" a voice suddenly asked Jackamara. I leapt a metre into the air and landed ready to dash away; but the voice was male. I relaxed as much as I could.

' "An Australian, a government man who might help our, your cause."

' "Is he, and can he?" the voice insinuated.

'I waited, contact had been, had been established. A coarse laugh came from the shadows and the voice directed itself at me: "And what is your name, Mr Australian?"

'I gave it. My confidence returned with a rush. The man spoke perfect English. Jackamara whispered that it was Lataoga and that he belonged to the ruling family. Well, I thought, it seemed that just about everyone, except us, did. The man stepped out of the shadows and I gave a start. He was naked except for a short piece of cloth about his loins. His hair was matted and worked up into an exaggerated coiffure so that it looked like his head was twice the size of that of a normal man.

'I wondered why this man would play the savage. He was a class above the inhabitants of Brooke's so-called authentic native village and I was sure that if he condescended to play a part in the new nation, tourists would just love to photograph the genuine article. My view was strengthened when we walked into a clearing filled with stilted, thatched huts with nary a sheet of tin on them. This, I knew, was the authentic Neo-Polynesian village just waiting for exploitation. "Come," the ersatz savage ordered. We went to a group of huts which were arranged in a circular traditional pattern.

'Lataoga informed me that he was the founder of this village of, what he termed, "free islanders". He stated: "Because I am family, they decided that I should become a minister of religion and thus be able to manipulate the island church. It is our, their way. They have to have a finger in everything. Even then I was clever, cunning, if you prefer. I agreed to go to a school in New Zealand. There, I learnt everything I could, not what they expected and more than they bargained for. There were many young people from the islands of the Pacific. Young men and women who were concerned about their traditions and customs being corroded away. I learnt much from them. We on these islands are virtual slaves. We work and get little in return. I came back from, from that period of exile an activist determined that my people should achieve a true independence which means freedom from exploitation and control over our own islands and lives. We want to establish a true Neo-Polynesian nation strong in custom and tradition."

' "Very commendable," I agreed dryly in the same stilted English he affected. I took advantage of a patch of shadow to give a quick smile. Politicians began this way, naive in the belief that they could change, or keep things as they were. Why, hadn't I almost become one myself? Hadn't I too the gift of the gab and the ability to waffle on with the best of them?

' "When independence arrives, I shall see that it is a real independence," he shouted out in controlled anger, hoping to make an impression on me. He flung a stick, which he had been holding, at a tree before resuming in an even, controlled voice. "This village," he explained, "is a return to Neo-Polynesian self-management and self-sufficiency. Our gardens are flourishing and we have a surplus which we trade in the town for what we cannot produce. We are setting up an alternative economy and a model administration which will eventually stretch throughout the islands. In many ways our so-called rulers are careless and we are able to bribe the captain of the schooner to take us to and from Fiji as crewmen. Sometimes though, we have difficulty in landing, for Fiji has what they call immigration control and they at times police it strictly."

'I nodded again, enjoying his role playing. I liked the bit about "what they call immigration control" as if he didn't know what it meant. He after all was an educated person and had been in New Zealand. He knew, he must know, all the ins and outs of a functioning modern country. In fact, he was closer to me than to his fellow islanders.

'We stopped in the very centre of the village, a circle surrounded by the huts. Jackamara disappeared. We were alone; but from the dwellings came snores to indicate that indeed there were inhabitants. I wouldn't have put it past Lataoga to have arranged all this for my benefit. In the middle of the circle stood a larger hut and that was where we were going.

' "Our meeting house, school and church," he curtly informed me. "Here we decide everything by consensus. We Neo-Polynesians have always practised basic democracy. I trust that you shall report this to your government. We are neither socialists nor communists. Come inside and sit, we have things to discuss."

'I sat down with this democratic leader who quickly filled me in on how things were run on the island and then what he wanted from Australia. He wanted the Australian Government's help in pressuring Britain to see that free and fair elections were held before they withdrew. His villagers had been instructed in the democracy of the ballot box and shortly cadres would travel throughout the islands to spread knowledge of the process. "Even now," he stated, "the first are ready to go. Wherever they go, they shall set up freedom villages for the islanders, just like this one and teach a return to the old tradition of group decision. The old Neo-Polynesian way of doing things is our way, our contribution to the democratic process, and it is but a short step upwards to form a national government based on the same principles."

'I nodded in the appropriate places. In asking for Australia's help, he had not mentioned what payment would be forthcoming. He must know that there is a price to be paid for everything; but it was not my function, as yet, to tell him what Australia might demand for its services, and by Australia, I meant myself, for I could see myself as the island expert supervising the elections.

'He continued his monologue into the night and I agreed with all that he said, having learnt that this was the best way of handling politicians. Agree and agree and when they stop for breath, put the boot in, though not this time. I couldn't help sneering also at his concept of group decision making. I well knew how groups could be manipulated to come to the right decision. Let each have a say, let them argue over and over about trivialities and points of order and at the end of the session when everyone was exhausted get them to agree without demur. A simple enough manipulation, and doubtless Lataoga knew it. When independence came he would be on top, placed there by all in a group decision. Well, that was only politics, and I believed in giving a bloke a fair go, especially when it would benefit me and allow me to get my own back on Carla. Now all that I had to do was write up my report, get to Fiji, send it to Australia and then get myself properly accredited to this island group. Lataoga was my ticket to the future. My mission had been accomplished and with it my rehabilitation, though I couldn't help wondering what Jack-amara was doing on the island, and when he would leave. Suddenly, my ebullient mood collapsed. How could I betray Carla who was the best, most beautiful and richest woman I had ever met? I wanted to share in her riches and power. Now Lataoga had given me a weapon to use in my campaign to gain her. Now I could play both sides against the middle and hope that I could gain her in the division of spoils.

'I promised to get all the details to Australia and after promising to arrange further meetings with him through Adaboaga, I left him and his model village of democracy to trek back to the mansion. I had plenty to think about during that moonlit scramble. I needed full accreditation to make my presence felt on the island. This should come now that I had established enduring contacts with both parties in the independence stakes, and what was more, was in the position to influence the race. Ah, the future was juicy with contracts and deals for me to arrange. If I played it straight down the middle and kept my cool, little could go wrong; but, but, I had to keep my emotions under control. I had to, or else I still might come a cropper. I had let Lataoga know that I was an intimate of the Prime Minister and often dined with the Chairman of the Australian Aid Development Commission. I had all but promised him a grant-in-aid. This meant profits all around and to me if handled rightly. I had hinted at this and noticed the gleam in his eye. Lataoga and I could do business.

'Ah, when I remember that hike back to the mansion and recall all that went through my head, I feel the power cursing through my veins. I held this group of islands in the palm of my hand and all that I had to do was close my fist to crush them into a nation of my own devising. I was flying high.'

SESSION TWELVE

'The mansion was as silent as a tomb as I pushed open the side door. I stopped and listened. Not a sound. I latched the door and crept up the stairs to my room. In the dawn's early light I undressed. I indeed did feel like a spy glowing in the knowledge of mission accomplished. Indeed, as I lay there with the sun rising above the horizon, I did feel like the accredited representative to this emerging nation. I dozed off in the official guesthouse.

'At breakfast, though I had had only a few hours of sleep, I was wide awake and could hardly keep the smirk off my face. Even Carla and Brooke's obvious intimacy and Miss Tamada's look of repletion did not spoil my mood. Indeed, I said to the Japanese woman, "You look like the fox which has got the chicken." To which she replied: "And you look like the man who followed the will-o'-the-wisp to an old broken skull.' " I smiled at her attempt at levity and devoted my attention to my plate heaped with bacon and eggs. I had at last got on top of them all and soon Carla would be coming to me. I knew it, and as for the Japanese woman and her damned corporation, well, rich pickings there, for sure.

'I felt so high and mighty with my victory that I was unprepared for any fall. Alas, I should have known that in this world, things do not work out so quickly or so well. I should have remained on guard; I should have made allowances for Carla's perverse sense of timing. You know those mixed breeds. Sorry, I'm not trying to offend you; but, well, put it down to the white blood in her. What, you see this as racism, directed against whom, I might ask, sir? It is I who should be offended, not you, for I was the victim of a devilish plot. A plot worthy of the talents of Fu Manchu. What, you have read the books and find them offensive? Well, so be it. Let me go on with my narrative. It is almost finished and I, I am growing tired of it. It is not a pretty story . . .

'Alas, I should have known that a clever and experienced woman such as Carla would counterattack. Carla and her Japanese companion had worked on my mind, manipulated and learned its methods of operation. They knew the alleys and roads. I was an open city to them, whereas, whereas, they were strange territory to me. I was only a businessman from the Gold Coast; I was a failed electoral candidate; now I am a civil servant. I am staid, unlike those who control our destinies. What, you want me to go on? I am, I am, though it will not be to add to the reputation or glory of that Dr Watson Holmes Jackamara.

'During breakfast, Carla launched her counterattack. "A contract is a contract and any breach shall be severely punished," she said incomprehensibly.

' "Any laxity on our parts might prove disadvantageous, if not disastrous," Brookes added, backing her up.

' "Knowledge is power, and not to know everything is to know nothing," she stated.

' "We have to show him, them, that our eyes and ears are everywhere," Brookes replied.

' "And that we are in business and that we mean business," Carla added, her pointed, pink tongue darting out to lick her luscious bottom lip.

'Miss Tamada couldn't help but put in her two cents' worth: "And what are ethics when our continued connection is at risk?"

'She wrinkled her nose at me, smiled at Carla, then at Brookes. I cursed under my breath, and knew that any deals I made with this woman would be hard and as tough as B.H.P. steel.

'Carla touched Miss Tamada's hand and let her fingers linger there as she smiled at me, then began to explain in the way she knew infuriated me. "You see, sweetness," she began, using the affectations of her female trade, "one of my uncles, by the way we are a prolific family as you may have found out by now, was one of the first anthropologists to engage himself in field work using strictly scientific methods based on linguistics, the theories of Saussure to be specific. Naturally, he did not wish to study some foreign people, but turned his attention on our very own islanders. His elaborate study, *The Metonymy of Punishment Among Five Neo-Polynesian Communities*, is considered a classsic in its field. Unfortunately, the original volumes are hard to find, even in university libraries. I dismiss the single condensed volume as beneath contempt, and if you really wish to understand his work you must find and read the ten-volume original edition which is arranged according to the metonyms employed and constructed from the punishments meted out. Well, seeing that we are so fortunate in having this entry into the minds of the islanders, we have devised a penal code according to their psychology decoded from their Neo-Polynesian traditions and customs." She stopped and smiled at me as she said this. I became uneasy. Lataoga had competition in the Neo-Polynesian stakes. She continued: "Needless to say they see incarceration as the most barbaric of all punishments and what we may term torture as the most appropriate way of dealing with those who transgress their laws. We accept custom and tradition in this matter and you will not find one prison on our islands. We are, after all, very traditional people . . . And perhaps, you may be wondering why I bring up this subject now, and at the breakfast table. Today, you are fortunate in being able to witness the punishment of a criminal. Adaboaga has been found guilty of offences which in Australia would be labelled treason. He was brought before a council of islanders and the charges were found to be proved. Naturally, we believe in the democratic process, though the processes of administration and the judiciary are not separate . . . "

'I tried to evade her voice as I felt my mood turning sour. Jackamara had been discovered, had been discovered, discovered, discovered; it echoed in my mind. I pulled myself together and forced myself to listen.

' "It is needless to add that my learned uncle wrote and

delivered before the Royal Society a paper entitled, 'The Function and Metaphor of the Governing Council in Neo-Polynesian Society', in which he proves that all government is subject to metaphor and contains within the council a hierarchical system based on the pronouns of the Neo-Polynesian language. He also saw that the council was an ideal governing instrument if one could exclude certain individuals desirous of manipulating members of the council desirous of being manipulated. He put down this attitude, or stress, as being due to the system of pronouns which necessitated an actor and an acted upon, an agent and a reagent, or indeed an agent and an anti-agent. But I suppose you know all about this?"

'The manager of the plantation could not hide his grin, nor could Miss Tamada. I glanced from him to Carla, to the Japanese woman and couldn't meet their eyes. I felt that I was guilty of the most flagrant, most flagrant—most, what? I wasn't guilty of anything at all. I was merely serving the interests of my country; and what is more as an accepted guest, I had every right to meet people. Then what had I to do with this Adaboaga/Jackamara and his crimes? He had entered the islands a spy, and, and well, he was to be punished according to their laws and as Adaboaga, not as Jackamara. His cover had not been broken. I decided to feign disinterest in the whole proceedings. I attempted a smile as I replied: "That's very interesting, but obtuse, Carla, though there does seem to be a grain of sense somewhere in it. I have been a member of a number of committees and can vouch for the way crass manipulation occurs. Why, I remember one Royal Commission in which the frames of reference . . . "

' "Yes, yes darling, but another time," Carla broke into what would have been a long narrative to get them away from the subject and Adaboaga. "Now," she went on, "there is the sentence to be carried out. This is another aspect of our culture which should interest you. The aggrieved party must carry out the sentence and as we all are the aggrieved party in this case, we shall be the ones to do it. Things are being readied and soon you'll have the opportunity to watch, though as a foreigner you cannot play the executioner; but you'll enjoy the execution, won't you, sweetness?"

'Suddenly, I felt myself returning to that paralytic state I had experienced at the time of my poisoning. My body lost all sensation; but my consciousness remained clear. I could neither agree nor disagree. My field of vision held only Carla. Her green eyes glittered ice into my soul. The slivers burnt there coldly. I gave a shiver as the state of paralysis left. White-faced, I gulped in air as I felt my chest move. I grabbed my cup of coffee and drank it down. They got up and meekly I followed them into a large barn standing a short distance from the mansion.

'The barn was empty; but a sturdy pole, planted into the ground, stood near the far wall. There were four iron stakes embedded in the concrete floor. Only the blunt ends through which holes were pierced were above the concrete. I thought they were used for securing unruly animals and such things. I wasn't really interested in them; but my consciousness had remained clear and took in every detail. Then my detachment received a shock as Elias led his manacled partner in. Today there was no booming laughter. His huge body seemed weak and powerless. I tried to make contact with Jackamara, but he refused to look at any of us as he submitted entirely to the ritual.

'Adaboaga/Jackamara allowed Elias to push his body face down on the floor between the four iron stakes. The manacles were removed and short hand and leg irons were used to fasten him down. It appeared a very professional job, and I shuddered as my mind made this observation, for what had I to do with such things? When did I ever have anything to do with such a thing? Lastly Elias ripped the clothing from him. Now, I thought, was the time to intervene; but I lacked the will to move. I could only stare down at the wretch spread-eagled before me. I managed to glance at Carla. Her eyes had glazed into a dull green, while her fingers curled and uncurled about the butt of a whip which had appeared from nowhere. Suddenly she cracked it. I leapt back.

' "Are you ready?" she hissed at me.

' "Am I ready?" I stuttered back, stupidly trying to evade the knowledge that she was offering the whip to me; but how could I whip a fellow human being, how could I . . . could I? Perhaps by doing so I might save him from being hurt too much; but I couldn't. I numbly shook my head and received a hysterical laugh and slurred words in return which I failed to decipher. She raised the lash and was beginning to bring it down, when I turned and ran from the barn. I couldn't stay to watch a fellow Aussie, though a black one, being flogged. Behind me I heard the lash strike. One, two, three, four, five, six, seven, eight. "Not so pretty now," I heard the demented woman shriek out. In my mind I was staring in horror at the red slashes cutting across the taut flesh, cutting into the taut flesh, at the skin finely cut, the bubbles of blood beginning to emerge and the pool of urine forming beneath the body. How I pitied Jackamara. What had he done to deserve such punishment? Sickened, I ran from the sounds. The thwack, thwack, thwack, thwack of the lash striking flesh forced me away to the very cliff edge.

'Even there I could hear the sounds of punishment and torment. A long screaming wail came from the hapless victim. It was the first of many. Thump, thump, thump, thump on the living vibrant flesh. On the surface of the sea, I pictured Carla's manic face as she used the long whip expertly, cracking the lash just above poor Jackamara's back. Each crack severed neatly a sliver of flesh; each crack heralded a scream, until there was nothing but the sound of that lash.

'I couldn't take it any longer and vomited into the sea. Then came blessed, blessed silence. I barely was conscious when Carla came and stood next to me. When did I bring myself to glance at her, I shuddered to see her hands and clothing all bloody. There was even blood on her cheeks and a trickle came from the corner of her mouth. I hugged my body to myself and began shuddering. My will had been well and truly broken. I had one wish and one obsession only—to get off the island and far from its savage inhabitants.'

SESSION THIRTEEN

'I'm sorry that I couldn't go on yesterday. Even now, even after years and with my knowledge, I still feel queasy, still feel on the verge of fainting. Yes, even now. It all seemed so real, though I know, I do, I do that it was most unreal, most unreal. But I'll go on, the worst is over, or is it? I still hear the thwack, thwack, thwack of that whip descending on, on, I never did see who, or what? Should I have done so, then I would have known, known for sure . . . Enough, enough, I stand on the cliff beside Carla. The day begins falling into the ocean. I feel disgust at her and her attraction for the grotesque—and the acting out of that grotesquery. She was sick and a throwback to her savage side which I had never thought could happen. How could such things still endure into the twentieth century? How could they exist on this island where Sas Enterprises had such an influence? Sas Enterprises was devoted to all that was beautiful and run by a woman who ventured into the depraved and foul. She had ripped the shroud of innocence from me. I existed in sin and guilt because I had done nothing to rescue Jackamara from their clutches. I had let a colleague be flogged to death. No one could have endured that long and awful punishment without succumbing.

'Even then, I did nothing. We stood looking at the end of the sun, that woman and I. The sky spurted blood, the blood oozing and dripping from the back of that wretched man. It became streaked with long, purplish bruises of surprising translucence. This was the bewitching hour when flowers assumed a mysterious brilliance, the last gasp of life before being plunged into the grave of the night. All around us flamed the brightness of decay and death. No, no, the brightness of hope and birth, of the new life that Lataoga would bring when he emerged from his jungle fastness. He would heal the sickness

122

and justice would flare up in all its light, and I would help him to bring about the necessary changes. But I didn't believe it; I never wanted to concern myself with this wretched island. Lataoga was a part of this awful family, of this awful island.

'I was so distraught that I took refuge in nature. I turned to the garden. The paths were strewn with powdered coral and marked out a square of sanity around a huge tree in which birds were squabbling and squawking in happy, normal life. It may have been a banyan tree, for roots fell to reach the earth from all the branches and formed a bower which repelled me. Then the birds suddenly stopped their noise and settled down for the night. Bats replaced them to wheel about in their geometric flights. A giant moth flew past in a perfectly straight line, his wings flapping and not fluttering. From the sky to the tree and from the tree to the sky reached a silence which filled me with a foreboding as soft and as velvet as bat wings edged with claws. It penetrated me, made me ache to be away where the buildings rose on all sides in straight lines of sanity. How I wished just to be in a disco, or in a restaurant. None of these existed on this island. I was lost in a savagery which mocked the whole concept of culture. And yet, and yet standing next to me was one of those fashion arbitrators of that culture. Yes, she belonged to Europe with its ordered cruelties and not to these islands where her family had imposed a mockery of civilised savagery. Poly-this and Poly-that; Neo-this and a Neo-that. Oh I was thinking too much and not about the right things. Shouldn't I have been seeking out the remains of Jackamara, really seeing what state he was in? But I couldn't, I couldn't. I was rooted to the spot, right next to that woman who had inflicted such pain and agony.

'I glanced to where she stood resting on the low, stone wall protecting us from the edge of the cliff and any flights of fancy we might have. Her back was towards me as she stared over the ocean which gleamed, dark and as lustrous as her hair, and far down and away from me. A last ray from the disappearing sun leapt out to strike the side of her neck and the emerald necklace which she wore blazed as brightly as her eyes. I watched her body relax in that green fire. I came to her and saw it playing over her features. I gazed into her face and saw that her blood-flecked lips were thinner. Nervously, her teeth gnawed at the bottom lip. I felt that I wanted to take her in my arms, make her forget all the hideousness which she had witnessed. And all at once, the air was filled with a host of fireflies. They fluttered about her in a sparkling halo of fire. Her face lifted and she appeared a Madonna. It was then that she spoke, spoke in a hushed voice which lingered on the recent bloody scene.

' "Love, we humans are truly astounding, we really are. And if there were other peoples living on the stars and they knew of us, just imagine how they must despise us. We have tamed the world and put nature into chains, and then, we have whipped her. We have artists and poets, we have aesthetic pleasures galore, but what we dote on most of all is pain and the inflicting of pain. How wonderful we are: the torturers of the universe. We torture, therefore we are. Is this not true, my Australian, you who belongs to a nation founded on torture, bloodshed and genocide?"

'Her nails raked my arm to gain my full attention: "Listen, listen," she exclaimed, "listen damn you! The blood of murderers, torturers and victims flow through your veins, accept them all, or pick one and rejoice." I couldn't move; I couldn't speak; I refused to countenance such things. "Please stay on my island," she implored. "I'll build fantastic pleasure gardens of horror. Please listen, please be kind to me. I need you—I really do."

'She turned away to hide her tears and her body shuddered. No, I believe now that it was from suppressed laughter. I don't know. I still don't, for the next moment she turned to me with insults: "How disagreeable you are; how old, weary and dreary. You never reach out for me, never take my hand. I've had enough. You're too cold a fish for my net. To think that I once fancied you . . ."

'At last I found my tongue and found myself stuttering out words in denial. On the verge of hysteria, in shock, over the edge; but she brushed me away with her own brand of emotion. "No, no, I don't, won't speak to you ever! You're a drag; you make me miserable; you make all of us miserable with your prevarications and lack of understanding."

'Her voice shrilled on and on in an irritating keening. It whined out through the darkness like the uncanny cry of a vulture. A servant padded near and switched on lights to illuminate the area in which she was attacking me. What could I do but take it from this, this creature? Her voice shrilled on through the warm air, but the light revealed her to me in all her perfection. I stared at her, but her voice grated on my nerves. Her eyes, her lips, her neck, the heavy, red hair which she was always threatening to blacken, the fires of her desires, even her riches repelled me. I had to move away from her side. Her attraction threatened me with, with annihilation. I stared down the open neck of her soiled blouse. The swell of her breasts beckoned. How I wished to bury my face there. My fists clenched and unclenched, unclenched to clench. My fingers writhed. I ached to choke the life out of her. I wanted to strike out at this woman who was reducing me to an insignificant worm. I couldn't control myself. I ran to her virtually frothing at the mouth. I grabbed her arm cruelly as she had done mine, and shouted out in a curiously high-pitched voice: "Shut up, shut up, shut up! No more, no more of this bullshit!"

'My fist swung around and appeared to collide with her face, though I felt no satisfying thump of fist on flesh. She fell to the earth. Her pale face shone up at me and her dark eyes flashed with scorn. Quietly, she murmured: "Go on, kick me, that's all you're good for."

'My rage vanished as quickly as the day had gone into the night. No sooner had it flared than it was extinguished. I felt ashamed at hitting a woman—as ashamed as when I had hit my first and second wives. I helped her to her feet, trying hard not to see the derision on her face. I knew that I was weak, weak, weak; but she had driven me to it. "Carla, Carla, Carla," I cried out, for I still loved this woman.

'She remained silent, neither turning towards nor away from

me. I felt I was part of the mist rising from the ocean. I became as silent as that mist rising up the cliff face, wreathing the flowers, blurring shapes until they turned into the outlines of scaffolds. I smelt the rank odour of blood and spilt body fluids; I heard the sound of a gecko calling, calling to its mate. I needed this woman, but I knew what chance I ever had was gone. In defeat, I said: "Let's go back to the house."

' "Yes," she agreed politely, "it is almost dinnertime." And when we entered the mansion, there came the cool tone of her voice asking: "Shall you be going to Fiji on the next boat? It gets in tomorrow?"

'I replied, "Yes." And that was the last time I ever spoke to her. My sojourn on the island was over; but don't stop the tape-recorder, there is more to come. More which will enlighten you to the strangeness and the manoeuvring which had gotten me into such a mess. All has not been revealed, and I, I shall reveal what I know. If this account is ever published, it shall be up to the readers to form their own conclusions. You see I had been set up . . . Yes, I had been; but I shall end this segment of my life, get it out of the way. It must be investigated.

'Perhaps, yes I assume that someone will read these memoirs and perhaps they will want to know, not about the illustrious Dr Watson Holmes Jackamara so much, but about what happened to that newly emerging nation. Did the islanders succeed in becoming truly independent with the help of the British and Australian Governments? Well, I'll tell you what happened and what does happen. I wrote a detailed report on Lataoga and his freedom movement, all of it including his ideas on basic democracy. I posted it from Suva to a box number which I had been given and waited for an acknowledgment while I lazed about in a resort in an effort to rebuild my shattered nerves. A curt reply summoned me to Brisbane. I arrived and was shunted off to the old capital at Canberra where I was debriefed and where it was emphasised that I was and would remain under the Official Secrets Act. They offered me this job and here I have remained in this decaying town which was once the capital of Australia. Goodbye to the heady deals of yesteryear. My nerves could not stand any kind of pressure. Still, it is not such a bad position, the houses are now quite cheap in Canberra, and I have a little business on the side; but I won't talk about that. Then, well, to get back to that newly emergent nation, Lataoga is the Prime Minister and Carla of the green eyes and now black hair is the Minister for Tourism, Foreign Affairs and Industry. Soon after Independence, both came on an official visit to Australia. I received a invitation to attend the opening function of their new Embassy in Brisbane. I managed to reach the new capital and was amazed at how it had grown. I got in a taxi to go the reception and then my nerve failed me. I could not bring myself to enter. I joined the crowd outside the gates. Brisbane then had not gotten over its new status and crowds inevitably gathered to witness the arriving dignitaries at such functions. I watched our Prime Minister arrive in his black limousine. With him was Lataoga and Carla, and, and Watson Holmes Jackamara, the newly appointed High Commissioner to their nation. I was astounded by this. How could this man that I had almost seen beaten to death be hobnobbing with his torturers, with his chief torturer? And then I saw the person he was escorting. It was Miss Tamada. It was then that I realised that these people in front of me, from our Prime Minister down, had engaged in a huge plot which had been my ruin. It had started from that campaign for electoral office into which I had been inveigled; Jackamara, who was supposedly my bodyguard, had furthered the campaign with his story of the *Gyinggi* woman. The Prime Minister was privy to the plot and had arranged everything including my sitting next to the two women on the flight. Both had played their parts. How deep had the plot gone? Were even my debts, which forced me to contest the election, a part of the process to bring me undone? Sir, I have been the victim of a plot the ramifications of which are immense. It is impossible for a mere person to understand. Governments are involved; corporations are involved, and I have been ditched, cast off and made to suffer this job in this decaying town. How can I escape? How can I re-establish my life and my fortune? I fear that it is impossible, their machinations have not only ruined, but discredited me.

'They done me in, mate. Again and again, they did me in . . . I notice that you have never, never ever spoken into that microphone you keep shoving in my face. You are part of the plot, aren't you? Speak up and into the microphone.'

'No!'

'How can I believe you, you who are the official biographer of this, this Jackamara? I'm sorry, I'm sorry, of the Dr Watson Holmes Jackamara who played a part in my downfall. Don't deny it, he was there from the beginning gathering rewards and awards, while ashes were being heaped upon my head. Why was he made High Commissioner? Why was he given this juicy post? Why wasn't I?

'Because, if you must know, although the former Prime Minister held you in high regard, he became concerned about your mental state. You were to be the chosen one; but to put it mildly you mucked up and came a cropper. You were supposed to be the counterweight to the Kitsune Corporation, and what did you do?'

'What, what . . . ?'

'You know that our economy was on the upswing, that we needed projects for our construction crews . . . If it hadn't have been for the Prime Minister's genius in shifting the capital to Brisbane, we would have been landed in a recession, and this would have been because of your clumsy handling of what should have been a simple enough assignment. You had everything going for you and you blew it!'

'But, but . . . '

'The Prime Minister had not realised the state of your health which appears to have deteriorated rapidly after your disastrous campaign for electoral office. To add to this, you succeeded quite early in the piece in alienating the woman, Carla. She found you detestable and despicable. She can be quite realistic when it comes to business; but she certainly did not take to you constantly lying to her.'

'But, but . . . there were attempts made on my life.'

'It appears that you made an enemy of the captain of the inter-island schooner. He is a Scot and Scotsmen are not ready to forgive and forget. Then, though this is only a surmise, you offended the crew by calling them "Lascars". You blundered from pillar to post.'

'But, but how do you know all this? How do you, mate? How do you?'

'I have interviewed a number of the people involved. As Jackamara's official biographer, I am most impartial and collate the facts from as many sources as possible.'

'But why, why was that, that Aborigine made the High Commissioner? Answer me that! Expose the facts! Your impartiality demands it. Your readers must know them.'

'Dr Watson Holmes Jackamara is an exceedingly accomplished man in his field. This made him High Commissioner material. He was also on intimate terms with Miss Tamada of the Kitsune Corporation whom he had met in India many years ago and continued to keep up the relationship when she came to Australia. Also, his appointment was requested by Prime Minister Lataoga. He also was a longstanding friend of the former Prime Minister who was quite fond of him and called him affectionately his "Jacky".'

'I still declare that it was a plot, a plot to discredit and annihilate me.'

'Perhaps, but if there was one, it was not against yourself. I can see that the Prime Minister made one of his rare errors in choosing you for such a delicate mission. Still, that is long in the past and should be forgotten. Now as to the matter of payment. You said that you desired cash?'

'Yes, yes . . . and is it all there? Still have some minor debts you see, and the job, a mere sinecure, doesn't pay nearly enough . . . but then I do keep my hand in with a few little speculations. I might be down, mate, but I'm not out. One day I'll regain my strength and then you'll see.'

'Yes, yes, then we'll see. I just hope that you take more care in future; but none of this is my concern. I wish to thank you for giving me your time. I must say that I did find your account frankly fascinating. It will certainly be an aid to me in illuminating the career of one of Australia's greatest native sons . . . '

'Listen, mate, I find your attitude offensive and as for that famous native son you are whitewashing . . . He needs it with his black skin and heart. I want to say that only a Royal Commission will satisfy me. Sir, there has been skulduggery. Yes, I declare, skulduggery, and it must be brought out. The people of Australia must know how their country is run and how foreign affairs are conducted. They must learn that I have been a victim of a plot vast in its ramifications.'

'Yes, yes. Please could you make out a receipt for the money. Make it out personally to me. That will do. Thank you, and goodnight and goodbye.'

'A Royal Commission, sir, that is what I want. A Royal Commission. Publish my account. Let the readers make up their own minds about the matter. I challenge you to lay these facts before the Australian public. I challenge you . . . '

THE END